D0111375

Scottish Local History

AN INTRODUCTORY GUIDE

David Moody

Published in Great Britain, 1986, by B.T. Batsford Ltd.
4 Fitzhardinge Street, London W1H 0AH

Published in U.S.A., 1990, 1994, by
Genealogical Publishing Co., Inc.
1001 N. Calvert Street, Baltimore, MD 21202

Library of Congress Catalogue Card Number 89-81512
International Standard Book Number 0-8063-1269-6
Made in the United States of America

CONTENTS

LIST OF PLATES

PREFACE

My thanks are due to the following:

My employer, East Lothian District Library, for allowing me leave of absence for research, and District Librarian Brian Gall for suggesting the need for a book of this type.

Mr Galbraith and advisory staff at the Scottish Record Office for providing background material and answering many queries.

Tony Seward of Batsford, whose suggestions improved the book immeasurably.

None of the above, of course, is in any way responsible for errors of fact or interpretation.

Tribute should also be paid to the staff of the National Library of Scotland Lending Services for their efficient work in locating books required by researchers. Their efforts are unseen by most but are an indispensable support to public libraries and through them to local history researchers throughout the country.

Permission to reproduce illustrations was kindly granted by the following: no. 1 – Trustees of the National Library of Scotland; nos. 2, 4 and 8 – East Lothian District Library; no. 7 – Crown copyright: Royal Commission on Ancient Monuments, Scotland.

Local history researchers have been referred to throughout the book as males, simply because repetition of 'he/she' was thought to be cumbersome.

It has been frequently necessary in this book to summarize in a few lines the history and functions of institutions which evolved over hundreds of years. Crude generalizations have therefore been made which should serve only as an introduction to a more detailed study of historical sources.

Full details of references given in shortened form in the text (e.g. I. D. and K. A. Whyte (1981) on p. 13 are given in the References section at the end of the book (p. 170).

Chapter One
INTRODUCTION

There has been no more favourable time than the present for the study of Scottish local history, and a variety of factors have contributed. Changes in local government in 1974–5 created new district and regional authorities which, being on the whole larger than their predecessors, have been able to establish record offices and libraries devoted to local history archives and research materials. Technical developments have helped – for example, the advent of microforms has made it possible to reproduce records relatively cheaply. Thirdly, among professional historians there have been changes in attitude favourable to the study of local history. Wars, international diplomacy and the deeds of kings and ministers are no longer given such prominent attention to the detriment of social and economic factors, and in this context the study of the local community and its inhabitants has ceased to be regarded as a parochial pursuit of musty antiquarians. In part the new outlook is doubtless a reflection of the fact that the United Kingdom is no longer an important world power – historians, as much as the subject of their study, respond to changing fortunes with changing pre-occupations. At the same time there has been in recent years considerable cross-fertilization between local history and other disciplines such as sociology and geography, both of which tend to analyse society through a detailed examination of a locality. The influence of methods used in the natural sciences, where the emphasis is upon the painstaking collection of data, also means that the project with the local horizon becomes a more attractive and manageable proposition.

As a result of these various trends, the study of local history, which traditionally concentrated on the monuments of the past, great castles and mansions, battles and the famous men and women who happened to have been born in a locality, has now blossomed in quite new areas. It is now an accepted part of school and college syllabuses at every level, and practised by an ever-increasing number of enthusiastic amateurs from a variety of backgrounds and interests.

It is hoped that this book can offer a sound introduction to the current state of the subject and accommodate a variety of tastes and abilities. Space has been given to the three main categories of interest: *fieldwork* (there are sections on archaeology, recording gravestones and buildings, oral history and place-name surveys); *collecting* (topographical prints, postcards and ephemera); and *written research.* An attempt has also been made to link the themes discussed to those aspects of local history which are closest to us – our families and their past, our houses, churches, schools and places of work. These immediate areas, which can be studied as self-contained topics, are used at the same time as introductions to wider aspects of local research.

Chapters Two and Three are concerned with how to set about finding relevant material. Chapter Two investigates public library collections and how they can best be exploited and Chapter Three archive repositories and their holdings of public and private records. These are followed by three thematic chapters: the first considers the study of the people and communities of the past; the second, in contrast, investigates their material remains – the buildings and artefacts which they have left as their memorial; and the third attempts to place both in the context of a human settlement, in the study of sources for the history of a village, town or parish and the influences that have shaped their growth. The final chapter deals with the important subject of writing up and publishing results.

The book also sets out to provide an introduction to effective research techniques – a subject which has too often been neglected by local historians. To believe that the sole requirement is knowledge of local records and their whereabouts is a great mistake: the result will not be a worthwhile contribution to history but dull antiquarianism of the type which has given local history a bad name in the past. A conceptual apparatus is essential for any successful human activity, and in this respect, today's local historian is fortunate in that, in addition to the traditional methodologies of history, he has at his disposal others, some of which are not available to the political or national historian. His favourable situation derives, oddly enough, from the restricted nature of local studies. For spatial restrictions bring the local historian, as already suggested, close to areas of concern to others, such as archaeologists and geographers, who are similarly confined by considerations of landscape, and have in their turn moved closer to local historians in recent decades in their emphasis on the interpretation of processes (which can then be applied to specific localities) in preference to descriptive studies. A narrow focus of another kind – on the community – typifies the sociologist and anthropologist, and here too the local historian can benefit.

This work will touch upon some of the relevant themes and models developed in these other disciplines. What it cannot do is to give more than passing reference to the conceptual apparatus involved, the intention being that the reader attracted to the general ideas mentioned can turn to the specialized literature, where he will find a detailed analysis of the possibilities and pitfalls of any particular approach.

In most circumstances a local study forms part of the source material for a more general economic or social history – as an example illustrative of a general trend. As such, the local historian will usually be at a disadvantage in that he is less equipped with comparative evidence from other settlements with which to illuminate his own. Obviously background reading can fill the gap to some extent and is essential for any serious student. Relevant titles are suggested in the course of this book and in the Further Reading and Information sections. This observation, however, is not intended to denigrate local history. At its best, its microscopic approach, its attention to detail and its exploitation of the different academic disciplines mentioned above can produce work of integral quality not dependent upon reference to a wider context. It can also, by its immediacy, bring the past alive in a tangible and demonstrative way not possible with the more abstract considerations of the political historian. The fact that one can see and touch the subject one is studying is the root of its appeal.

Study techniques

Various points of historical methodology are discussed at relevant points in the text, but as a preliminary a few basic rules can be considered here.

Note-taking is a fundamental discipline about which there may appear to be nothing to say that is not self-evident, yet many mistakes are made even at this level, with disastrous consequences for all subsequent steps in a research project. Notes should not be made in notebooks, nor on the backs of envelopes or scraps of paper; loose-leaf sheets are the only sensible and versatile format, and they should preferably be large size (A4). Only with loose-leaf sheets can notes be manipulated effectively, and small formats encourage bad habits that militate against clarity. Note-taking should also be integrally structured around the materials under consideration, with each sheet headed with details of the source (book or document) being scrutinized. Full bibliographical details should be given on the first sheet, abbreviations on any subsequent sheet (one side only of the page should be used so that notes can later be cut up), and for each new source used a new sheet should be started.

It is true to say that a piece of research is rendered almost useless if the sources used in its compilation are not indicated in one way or another, and the actual forms of *citation* should be as follows (see the Further Reading section of this book, starting on p. 154, for examples. For books, the information should be taken from the title page, not the cover. First comes the name of the author(s), surname first, followed by forenames; next the title of the book and then the publisher (whose name usually appears at the foot of the title page – do not confuse the publisher with the printer); finally comes the year of publication, which is given either on the title page or on the following page, after the copyright symbol ©. Inclusion of the publisher is optional; date is more important (it facilitates quick identification of bibliographical tools in which other researchers and librarians can find the full details).

For journal, magazine and newspaper articles, the author and title of the articles are followed by the name of the journal, its volume number if there is one, the year, the part or month of the year if there is one and finally inclusive page numbers.

For documents and other archive material (for the distinction between these and books, see page 33) citation is given in a different way. First should come the name of the institution where the document is located – there is nothing more frustrating than reading about some records only to find that the author does not tell you where they can be found. The abbreviated name of the institution is followed by the title of the archive or its inventory code as given in the inventory of the institution concerned, and finally by the specific code number which uniquely identifies that document.

Note-taking is not a random or comprehensive transcription from the documents or books you are consulting at any one time. Such an activity is not only wasteful, but unstimulating. In research, you must pursue a clear purpose: the study of history is not the accumulating of facts about the past – it is asking questions about the past. Facts are only useful if they help you to answer the questions you have raised. Your notes, therefore, must be correspondingly structured: starting with questions, continuing with the accumulation of evidence, and finishing with conclusions. Your notes should be set out rather like reports of school chemistry experiments.

In this context it is easy to appreciate the importance of citations. If you do not give corroboration for the information you are quoting, it is equivalent to a scientist claiming that 50 per cent of deaths are due to the consumption of cream cheese but refusing to say on what evidence the claim is based. We would not take much notice of such a scientist. The lack of citations in a piece of work is another reflection of the antiquarian view of local history as a collection of facts. If you are not making claims (i.e. asking and answering questions) you are less likely to see the necessity of supporting them.

Given the discipline and single-mindedness which should characterize the researcher, he should be quite ruthless in the pursuit of his goals and the *elimination of superfluous endeavour*. He should therefore certainly not read every book relevant to his study from cover to cover: rather he should mentally tear them apart to get at the (perhaps) only two or three pages that are of value to him at that time – a task made easier through a full exploitation of book indexes. Similarly, when consulting documents, he should not be deflected by interesting but irrelevant byways. For documents and archives, one will not usually have the benefit of an index, so it is doubly important to cultivate rigorous and purposeful research methods, together with techniques of skimming rapidly through material until relevant passages are reached.

The historian's *questioning* occurs on several levels simultaneously. On the broadest scale, he is asking why things have changed in the way they have; but within this framework he formulates specific questions, both of the material he is using (is it logically argued? is it based on sound and extensive data?) and the information which it contains (how does it fit into the established consensus, and will that consensus need to be modified in the light of his investigations?). Above all it is important not to regard the records of the past as history, waiting like ripe plums to be plucked. Records are records; history is constructed by historians, like lumps of stone to be transformed into sculptures by a combination of hard work and imagination. When enthusiastic beginners become quickly disillusioned it is because they have not understood these basic principles.

Imaginative techniques are particularly important in Scottish local history because of the paucity of the surviving record. For many localities, there will be hardly any substantial written records before the sixteenth or seventeenth centuries, and this can lead to disappointment. It ought not to, if history is not thought of in terms of facts: the history of a parish is not necessarily incomplete if it has not included 'facts' from the thirteenth century, for example. By formulating different kinds of questions – those for instance posed by physical remains rather than written records – different answers can be obtained. True, we cannot say of such societies that such and such an individual lived there, but we can draw general conclusions about social and economic organization. The secret, of course, is to know what are the right questions to ask – with that knowledge, we will not suffer the kind of disappointment that amateurs sometimes feel. It is the ingenuity of the historian and the challenge he finds in handling different kinds of material which is the essential element in success, and which can make historical study an exhilarating experience.

Given the variety and scope of local studies today, you might consider joining a *local group* or *society*, which can harness the different skills of its members to a common end. As an example, a seemingly straightforward operation such as an archaeological excavation will today include on its professional team chemists, botanists, geologists, computer programmers, engineers – there is hardly a discipline which will not be involved somewhere. And local studies are very similar to archaeological excavations in this respect, all facets of the locality being illuminated by the specialist skills of different local inhabitants.

Local groups include the traditional antiquarian societies, societies covering special areas of interest (such as the Scottish Labour History

Society), and groups that come together for a specific project (oral history groups for instance). Names of relevant groups are given in the Further Reading and Information sections on pages 154–69 – information about those in your locality can be obtained from your local library. A complete list for Scotland is maintained by the Mitchell Library in Glasgow. In this book, addresses are only given where a society has a semi-permanent location. In other cases, names of office bearers tend to change frequently and addresses quickly become out of date. You should be able to get any information you require from your local history library or the Mitchell Library (telephone: 041 221 7030).

A final piece of advice concerns the *literature* of local history studies. There has been a relatively large output over the last few years, and some traditional works that have stood the test of time. But in the main they deal with *English* local history, even though they do not always indicate this in their title or elsewhere. Scotland, of course, was a separate nation up to 1707. It had, and still has, a completely distinct legal system and local government structure, and its social, economic and political history is markedly different from that of its neighbour. For these reasons, books on English local history are confusing for Scottish researchers, and their use should be restricted to those interested in comparative studies or ideas on methodology. In one or two specific areas, such as family history research, there has been a separate literature for Scotland, but apart from these the number of sources in not large. The most general guide yet produced is by I. D. and K. A. Whyte (1981), which the researcher is strongly recommended to consult. Articles on specific themes have appeared in the *Local Historian*, by I. H. Adams (1976) and R. Mitchison (1974) for example, and latterly in a new journal, *Scottish Local History*. Though some of the information is now out of date, *Local History in Scotland: Report of a Residential Course at Carberry Tower*, University of Edinburgh, Department of Adult Education, 1965, is still a useful guide, particularly the checklists of useful local records compiled by T. C. Smout.

This book is intended to help alleviate the shortage of source guidance and to enable the researcher to make an initial assessment of the records, institutions and themes that might be relevant to him to get his project launched with some degree of confidence. From that point on, his curiosity and enthusiasm will be his best ally, together with the works of generations of Scottish historians who can illuminate for him the context of his study. Hopefully, all those who dip into this book will feel encouraged to move on to further studies, and be rewarded with a deeper understanding of their local landscape and their forebears who moulded it.

Chapter Two

THE PUBLIC LIBRARY AND ITS COLLECTIONS

This book hopes to show that the study and writing of local history is well within the grasp of any amateur and does not require inordinate expenditure of time, money or energy. There are, it is true, useful institutions that may be a long way from your home, but this chapter in particular concentrates on those sources which are on your own doorstep, but none the less provide potential for exciting and original projects. Most of us after all have full-time jobs and the amount of time left to cultivate our interests is limited. Even if you are retired or unemployed, it may be a tall order to make frequent trips to Edinburgh where many of the records are kept. If you live in the central belt you are fortunate in this respect, but if in Dingwall or Dumfries you are at a distinct disadvantage and must look instead to resources available in your own town.

Your greatest ally in this endeavour is the public library, in the first instance your local branch or travelling library which can procure for you not only the material held by the local library authority, but books, photocopies and information from every part of the country through the inter-library loan service. Your interest in local history may have been fired in the first place by a specific circumstance – the discovery of an old ruin or artefact, a family document or photograph – or it may be a general interest generated by reading an article or book or moving to a new area. Whatever the stimulus, the biggest error you can make at this stage is to formulate too precisely the research project you intend to carry out. There are various reasons for this recommendation: firstly, you do not know what material is going to be easily accessible – in other words research projects must be geared to availability of data, not vice versa; secondly, you do not know if the material you want even exists (as we have suggested already, there is a problem with Scottish records in this respect); and thirdly, you do not know the potential of the subject or locality in which you are interested. The beginner often underestimates the variety and scope of local studies, and indeed often makes the fallacious assumption that there is only one option available to the local historian – the history of a locality, more often than not resulting in a poor, derivative piece of work regurgitated from other published sources.

Before you make a start, therefore, you should investigate three things: the basic records and sources pertaining to your area, their location, and the general background of your subject or locality. The last named can be achieved without going further than your local library: if you have been inspired by a specific circumstance you can obtain a thematically related item – for example a guide to Scottish genealogical research or a history of Scottish building; if your interest is general, you can look at one or two general histories of your area or subject, be it poor law, agriculture or economic history. At this stage you do not need to know specific authors and titles: your local librarian will be trained to do this work for you. Later on you may want to use bibliographies and library aids yourself, but at the start rely on the expertise of those accustomed to using them.

To answer your other two questions, your best course of action is to pay a visit to or telephone your local history library, which will probably be situated in the main central library in urban areas and the county town in rural areas. Explain that you are keen to become involved in local research, and would like advice on the parameters of possible themes. On the basis of what you are told, you may find you can make considerable progress researching at home with borrowed material. Depending on your circumstances you may have no realistic alternative, but given good advice and the right materials, a worthwhile project can develop even in these limited conditions. However, in most cases you will want to spend time researching at the local history library, beginning with a browse round its collections (which will normally be for reference purposes only, though there may be loan copies of many of the more popular items available from you local branch library). As you browse, read bits and pieces here and there, asking yourself questions and making a note of them. Some of them may not be fruitful when you come to look more closely, but at this stage your mind should be doodling and throwing up suggestions at random. For the more ideas you collect, the richer will be your study when you begin your research in earnest. It is only when your ideas have crystallized and you have specific goals to pursue that you should begin to collect relevant data: it is a waste of time to start with the facts before you have any inkling of the purpose for which you want them.

There are four main categories of material which you can expect to find in your local history library: books and journal articles, maps and plans, photographs and prints and, lastly, ephemera. Each of these categories will be looked at in turn, with the exception of maps and plans, which are discussed in Chapter Six.

Books and journal articles

The book collection will form the core of the local history library, as you might expect. What might surprise you however is the range of material that you can be faced with. The subjects covered will include: flora and fauna, geology, geography, folklore, industry, law, biographies of local men and women, genealogy, religion, architecture, social life, diaries, sermons and the published works of local authors. The arrangement of these books will usually be a twofold one: the primary division will be on the basis of locality (in rural areas the different towns and parishes; in urban areas the suburbs, though sometimes a system of dividing up the town by numbering grids is used). Within this division, the books will be subdivided according to their subject. The catalogue, traditionally on cards, now sometimes on microfiche, will list all the books under author and title.

A vitally important work the local centre will certainly possess (and which will probably also be available for loan) is the *Statistical Account of Scotland*, which is the local historian's most heavily used item. It was published in the last decade of the eighteenth century and is the most detailed economic and social record of parishes since the Domesday Book (which of course covers England only). It owes its origin in part to the agricultural reforming movement and was compiled by Sir John Sinclair from returns sent to him by the ministers of each parish, to discover 'the quantum of happiness enjoyed by its inhabitants and the means of its future improvement'. Depending therefore on the nature and interests of the minister concerned, the information ranges from the voluminous to the scanty. It is however likely to include at the very least a breakdown of occupations, details of local trade and industry, prices, names of major landowners and local monuments, as well as information on agricultural improvement. As each return was received it was made ready for publication, with the result that each volume contains a rag-bag of unrelated parishes, a disadvantage rectified in a recent reprint of the whole series, which now appears by county. Such was the impact of the *Statistical Account* that a second (known variously as the *New Statistical Account* or *Second Statistical Account*) was prepared in the 1830s and 1840s; this was published from the start in a county arrangement. A *Third Statistical Account* was undertaken after the second world war, but problems of finance resulted in erratic publication: some volumes were published in the early 1950s, while others are still appearing (with some information updated from that originally collected). The Third Statistical Account has larger thematic introductory sections than the previous two. The three together can be used in the comparative study of any parish over the last two hundred years, and can, conjointly with other records to be discussed in later chapters – census enumeration books, valuation rolls and local development plans – form a statistical framework for a wide variety of projects.

Many regions of Scotland boast local antiquarian or local history societies which produce transactions or proceedings, usually in annual volumes. There will be sets of these in the library, hopefully indexed so as to permit quick access to articles of relevance. The volumes also often contain valuable transcripts of public and private archives. Other sets of journals may be held, such as the *Proceedings of the Society of Antiquaries of Scotland* (dealing with archaeology) and the *Transactions of the Royal Highland and Agricultural Society of Scotland* (concerned with farming). The latter date back to the eighteenth century and, despite the title, cover all areas of Scotland. Other articles of interest may well be held in the form of photocopies from a wide range of journals, both old and new. These range from the technical and scholarly to the anecdotal and pictorial.

Travellers' accounts and tales give an interesting insight into local life from the outside and can often be more enlightening than official records. An interesting project would be to compare accounts given at different periods of your locality's history, though it must be remembered that travellers are by no means immune to bias or inaccuracy. The stock figure of the barbaric highlander for example recurs monotonously, though one can of course make these very preconceptions and misunderstandings the subject of the study. All travellers' accounts published up to 1900 are listed in Arthur Mitchell, *List of Travels and Tours in Scotland 1296–1900*, Society of Antiquaries of Scotland, 1902 (reprinted from volume 36 of their *Proceedings*).

Diaries similarly give an intimate flavour of local life, and Scottish examples have been published in two volumes edited by J. G. Fyfe (1927 and 1942). Many others appear in volumes published by historical societies (see pp. 20–23) and can be traced through W. Matthews, *British Diaries: an Annotated Bibliography of British Diaries Written Between 1442 and 1942*, Cambridge University Press, 1980.

In the exploitation of the local history library book stock, one point to establish clearly in your mind is the distinction between *primary* and *secondary* sources. A primary source is a contemporary record of events or attitudes; a secondary source (which can in some cases also be contemporary) is an interpretation of the significance of these records. Your own work comes in the latter category. The distinction is important because the two types of material are handled in different ways.

Primary sources can take many forms: they can be legal documents (house deeds, wills), archives (the administrative, executive or judicial records of institutions – the subject of the next chapter) statistics (account books, censuses), ephemera, oral recordings and field study reports (such as those from archaeological excavations). Maps, plans and photographs are primary sources; indeed the term covers anything which records as opposed to interpreting. Their value to the historian lies in the fact that they constitute his raw material; and in contrast to secondary sources he can on the whole trust the information which they present. The issue is not absolutely clear-cut: for example many contemporary records, even official records, can be misleading by omission or through the shared prejudices of a group or class. A newspaper is a contemporary source and a primary source, but there is a big difference between the way in which the historian will treat the advertisements or births' column and his approach to the editorial or reports. The first category can be basically trusted to give accurate information (give or take a printing error or two); the second obviously is already on the road to being a secondary source – an interpretation of events. An editorial in particular is quite clearly a secondary source. Yet at the same time it *is* a primary source in so far as it tells us the contemporary *view* of an event or situation. What of course is of the utmost importance is that you are constantly aware of the two different ways such records must be approached, depending on whether you are exploiting the primary or the secondary content.

These strictures apply equally, if not even more strongly, to those books and journal articles which are undoubted secondary sources. (Note that secondary sources may all be books, but not all books are secondary sources: some are transcripts of archives, some comprise visual material, some are statistical compilations.) A secondary source sets out both to describe and explain, a process essentially involving the making of judgements on questions ranging from the purely technical (e.g. dating a building from the style of construction) to the highly abstract (debates on the causes and consequences of events). In either case it should be apparent that you need to use secondary sources much more cautiously than primary sources, and in a different way, analogous to the distinction made above between the two ways of looking at a newspaper. A primary source is safer to use: it may be subject to error, but not to the perpetuation of unsubstantiated assumptions.

The beginner in local history sometimes thinks of his task exclusively in terms of the study of secondary sources, which is not only negative and unproductive, but also liable to cause disappointment. For the chances are that, contrary to a quite irrational expectation, there may well not be anything published on the locality or subject in which he is interested. Over-reliance on secondary sources stems from a passive view of the historian's role (fostered by bad educational methods at school) which sees them as fair game for indiscriminate plagiarism. But there can be no more pointless activity than regurgitating the results of others' researches except in the pursuit of examination qualifications. The true value of secondary sources lies elsewhere, notably in the framework they can provide for understanding the context in which to study primary sources (of course if they do not tally, it is the secondary sources which are wrong, not the primary sources) and in the corroborative or peripheral evidence they can supply to a researcher who is prepared to take their findings on trust but with a view to incorporating them in a different context.

The crucial decision whether or not to take any particular secondary source on trust involves a judgement based on the following criteria. Firstly, it should base its argument on data drawn as much as possible from primary sources (just as you in your turn should make it your aim to use primary sources too). A secondary source merely culled from other secondary sources is prone to perpetuate myth and falsehood, and though it may contain original flashes of insight or bring together information from a wide variety of sources, it will not in the main have contributed much to historical knowledge. Unfortunately there are many such books in the local history field, and any local history librarian will be able to give you examples of stories passed from one source to another down the generations without anyone actually trying to check the facts. A second criterion for judging a secondary source is that it should clearly indicate what data it is discussing and where it came from (through source references, footnotes or acknowledgements within the text) and should show the evidence leading up to the conclusion reached.

Perhaps a very large number of the local history books you will find on your public library shelves will not match up to these standards. Many of them, especially the traditional nineteenth-century histories of towns and parishes, give no source and present no thesis – they are antiquarian in a negative sense. There is often no organization of the facts, and no argument, and as such they are not illuminating secondary sources, but merely repositories of miscellaneous pieces of information. In other cases they are more in the nature of transcriptions of traditions and oral memories, very valuable as such, but not really what they purport to be.

Another difficulty for the modern researcher in using traditional secondary sources lies in the changing view of what constitutes local history. The nineteenth-century tendency was to see it in terms of great national and political events that occurred in one's locality or the involvement of local magnates in national or political affairs. You will therefore find what you thought was going to be a history of your own town turns out to be a detailed account of the administration of Mary Stuart, with perhaps one or two paragraphs, relegated to the last chapter, on 'civic antiquities'. The study of history at that time was seen as an ennobling occupation with ethical undertones. Thus the emphasis was on the example of 'great men' – warriors, politicians and writers (not the typical people of their generation). Today historical study tends not to attach so much importance to the leader, and the aim is to understand, not to inspire. We do not see the individual acting in a vacuum, but as part of a community or economic group; and we find the struggles and achievements of ordinary people as interesting and as valid a subject for study as the great. In this respect, as already mentioned, historical studies have been greatly influenced by other academic disciplines – geography in the emphasis on understanding how and why settlements develop, sociology in how communities operate, and economics in the causes of growth and change.

The result of these changes is that an historian today approaches the subject in a different way. He is more likely to choose a less general theme, socially rather than politically orientated, analytical rather than descriptive; and to compose a small vignette or cameo, a spark of light illuminating a particular area, problem or struggle. The researcher's broad study will be based upon a whole series of local studies of this kind – in a sense nearly all historians today are local historians. The problem for you is that your local library may have its shelves full of the biographies and works of famous sons of the town or county and of dull political histories, none of which will seem very relevant to the study you have chosen. But that is the challenge: ideas are always changing, and it is for you to contribute according to your own conception of historical study, moulding the primary sources available to you to that end, just as the historian of previous times interpreted them according to his requirements.

The limited scope of some parts of local history library collections reinforces the advice given at the start of this chapter: not to choose your subject of study first and then expect the institutions to come up with the right materials. You are likely to end up with a half-baked piece of work, but it is yourself you should blame, not the institution. There is a particular tendency to look much too narrowly at the potential of the subject – to think in terms of large periods of time and large nebulous subjects such as the history of a village or church. For a beginner these are much too grand, and quite honestly the work you produce in this respect will probably be trite, patchy and boring. This is a pity, for it is not due to a lack of ability or imagination on your part, or of potential in the collection you are using. Instead, consider following some ideas that play to the strength of your institution. In the case of your local history library you could for example look at the literature of your town or county, either compiling a trail of landmarks with literary associations or investigating the depiction of the locality in novels – the way writers have reacted to its landscape and inhabitants. You could turn to the volumes of sermons by local ministers and study the changing religious and social message, perhaps even relating them to specific local events. You could examine the folklore and legends of your district and their development, asking yourself what religious or social functions they performed. Some regions boast magnificent collections of tales, such as Wilson's *Tales of the Borders*. If you are interested in this type of literature, you might also like to look at the collection of chapbooks in the National Library of Scotland.

Published archives

In many cases the archives of public and private institutions will not be found in the public library but in record offices, both local and national. However, your library is likely to hold published transcripts of some of them, and will be able to borrow others through the inter-library loan system. The publishing of transcripts began in the early part of the nineteenth century when historians first became aware of the importance of archives, and the programmes have continued down to this day. Unquestionably from the local historian's point of view, it is always preferable to use a published source, for three reasons at least. Firstly, it was the traditional policy in Scotland to centralize records in the Scottish Record Office, where their use is not always convenient for the amateur researcher (it is closed in evenings and at weekends for example). Secondly, the original documents, particularly those from earlier periods, will be difficult to read because of the enormous differences in handwriting and spelling; some indeed will be in Latin, medieval Latin at that, and unless you are a specialist you will be able to make no headway at all. Which brings us to the third point, that the published version will have been edited by a scholar. He may have made a translation, he will have included copious notes explaining the significance of different passages and terms used, and he will have written an introduction setting the documents into a general context.

The Scottish Record Office have published many of the national archives of Scotland, but the main contributors to record publication have been societies constituted expressly for that purpose. Some have had a general remit: the Scottish History Society for example was set up in 1887 for the 'discovery and printing, under selected editorship, of unpublished documents illustrative of the civil, religious and social history of Scotland'. Of similar character are the Scottish Record Society, founded in 1897 as the Scottish section of the British Record Society but becoming independent in the following year, and the defunct Bannatyne (1823–61) and Maitland Clubs (1828–59). Others have specialized: the Scottish Burgh Records Society (1868–1908) produced a valuable series including burgh charter and minute books; and thematic specializations have distinguished the Stair Society (law), the Wodrow Society and Scottish Ecclesiological Society (religion). Some societies have had a regional bias (Grampian Club, Spalding Club).

Records transcribed include court books (sheriff, commissary, barony and justice of the peace), minute books of various bodies such as commissioners of supply, presbyteries and trade incorporations, charter books, estate rentals, household accounts, muniments (documents preserved as evidence of rights or privileges), writs (legal notices and agreements), letters (the earliest Scottish survivals being from the sixteenth century), diaries and business papers. They can be reproduced in different degrees, the main categories being as follows.

A *transcript* is a full text.

A *calendar* is a précis, usually in English, full enough for most purposes to replace the original documents.

A *list* is an enumeration of items composing a class of records, with minimal descriptive information. In most cases it will need to be used as a finding tool alone.

A *descriptive list* is a list with brief abstracts of the documents.

An *index* is an alphabetically arranged guide to people, places or subjects in the records. For genealogical research, an index entry may provide all the information needed, but for most other purposes it will, again, be used as a finding aid.

A *catalogue* is a calendar, list or descriptive list containing items from different origins but on similar subjects, or in the hands of a specific institution or individual.

It is quite important when considering possible subjects of research that you assess the availability of published archives. Initially you can consult Charles Sandford Terry, *A Catalogue of the Publications of Scottish Historical and Kindred Clubs and Societies 1780–1908*, Maclehose, 1909 and its successor, Cyril Matheson, *A Catalogue of the Publications of Scottish Historical and Kindred Clubs and Societies 1908–27*, Milne & Hutchinson, 1928. A summary bibliography of all publications up to 1954 is given in the *Handlist of Scottish and Welsh Record Publications*, British Records Association, 1954. For the period post-1954 you need to rely on general Scottish bibliographies (discussed on pp. 30–31) and on catalogues produced by the record societies themselves. The Scottish Record Society, for example, publishes a periodically updated list of its publications, and Scottish History Society titles are to be found at the end of each published volume. Even these bibliographies do not exhaust the field, for your own local antiquarian society may have published some records in their volumes of transactions.

As well as traditional forms of transcription, there has appeared in recent years a new development, which promises to extend quite considerably the possibilities for local research. The advent of microforms, most often encountered in the form of microfilm (in a long strip) or microfiche (on a card approximately 15 cm × 10 cm) harnesses photographic technology to provide a cheap and compact reproduction of original documents. The difference from the traditional methods is that you see a facsimile of the original record. The disadvantage is that you do not have the guidance of an editor. Still, for most purposes it is preferable to be able to use the records at leisure in your locality rather than have to make a visit to a possibly distant depository. There is less pressure of time, and less danger too for the documents themselves. If you are not acquainted with microforms, have nothing to fear – they are not an example of complex modern technology, unintelligible except to the initiated. Rather they are pieces of film with miniature photographs of text recorded on them. The machines used to read them – microfilm and microfiche readers (some machines combine both and can even include a photocopier) – are simply magnifying glasses with a light behind them and a knob to twiddle the film up and down. You can master them in three minutes. The categories of record that have been reproduced in microform are varied. Some projects have been carried out by large institutions producing multiple copies of the archive concerned; but it is equally possible to make just one copy, and your own library authority may well have commissioned its own programmes, both from its own holdings of rare or bulky material, and of records from elsewhere. So it is not possible to generalize about what microform material you will find in your area. Newspaper files are a common choice, as are valuation rolls and genealogical records, the latter being especially associated with the Mormon Church, which has reproduced the enumeration books of nineteenth-century censuses and the entire series of old (pre-1855) parish registers.

A recent experimental publication that is a possible pointer to the future is the compilation of the records relating to one locality: *Records of a Scottish Village: Lasswade 1650–1750.* Included are Poll Tax returns (giving information on size, structure and wealth of the population), the Parish Register of Births, Marriages and Deaths, and testimonials (certificates of good behaviour for those entering or leaving the parish). The collection was published by Chadwyck-Healey in 1983.

Today in the local history library, emphasis is very much on the acquisition of other kinds of primary sources in addition to those we have just discussed. Examples are current printed council minutes, electoral registers, files of local newspapers, census material, local plans and planning reports, valuation rolls, and annual reports of local institutions; such that future generations are going to be well served in respect of records of local life today. Also collected is a range of material of a less substantial nature, known as ephemera – posters, programmes, menus, church and school magazines, bill-heads, political leaflets – the list is virtually endless. Some material of this kind has always been collected by libraries – photographs and prints, directories, yearbooks and almanacs, broadsheets and town and county guide books.

Collecting local history material – antiquarian books, postcards and ephemera – is an activity you might wish to undertake yourself, and quite original collections can be made without necessarily spending any large sums of money. Potential projects are mentioned in the ensuing pages: here a few of the main categories of collectables are considered – newspapers, photographs and prints and ephemera.

Newspapers

The first Scottish newspapers appeared in the middle of the seventeenth century, but none had any lasting stability until the foundation of the *Edinburgh Evening Courant* and the *Caledonian Mercury*, in 1718 and 1720 respectively. These were national newspapers; a provincial or regional bias was first evident in the *Glasgow Journal* (1741) and the *Aberdeen Journal* (1748). News from around the world (often of the 'curious' rather than informative kind) was featured, but there were also many advertisements and a little local and commercial news. The advertisements, a miscellany of (in the words of R. M. W. Cowan (1946)) 'property sales, lost dogs, entertainments, medicines, functions, clothing, language tuition and rudimentary cosmetics' remain the most valuable part of a local newspaper for the historian until the mid nineteenth century.

The first substantial local news coverage appeared in the *Glasgow Mercury* (1778) and comprised (Cowan again) 'vital statistics of several districts, presbytery and circuit court reports, and details of the examinations of the Grammar School of Glasgow . . .'. The ferment of the French Revolution, followed by the movement for electoral reform, led to a considerable expansion of the newspaper industry – Edinburgh alone for example boasted seven newspapers at the beginning of the nineteenth century. Local reporting was still not prevalent, though this was not always the fault of the newspaper: some town councils, for example, met in camera. The modern form of the local newspaper evolved in the mid nineteenth century, with reports and some comments upon local events, obituaries of local worthies and less emphasis on the coverage of national and international news. For the local historian the newspaper is a rich and varied source: the family historian can profit from the columns of births, marriages and deaths, the advertisements tell us about shops, prices and the articles of daily use, the letters from readers give the flavour of local opinion, the photographs (which start to appear in our own century) present a visual record of people and places, and the newspaper articles themselves cannot afford to be neglected by anybody interested in the history of sport, social life, local politics and industry.

Locations of newspaper files are listed in J. P. S. Ferguson, *Directory of Scottish Newspapers*, National Library of Scotland, 1984. The National Library of Scotland also publishes a list of its own holdings in its *Current Periodicals*, which is updated from time to time. Your local history library is certain to have some files – the extent will probably depend upon the antiquity of the library authority concerned, the larger burghs usually being best provided. However, in recent years, by means of microfilming projects, many libraries have made good some of their deficiencies. In some cases the best runs are held by the newspaper offices themselves; this can be limiting, as facilities for consultation are often poor and, whatever the helpfulness of the staff, their main priority is to produce their daily or weekly newspaper.

Many of the files held by libraries will have been indexed in varying degrees of depth. Some indexes cover only personal names as found in announcements of births, marriages and deaths; while at the other extreme there are those whose detail extends to recording all subjects and individuals mentioned in the text articles, and even names of classified advertisers.

A distillation of news items can be found in scrapbooks of cuttings compiled either by library staff, or by local history enthusiasts who have subsequently donated them. Scrapbooks can be fascinating pot-pourris of curious information – the best will include other material too (addresses to the electorate, satirical leaflets, souvenirs of ceremonial events). If you want to compile one yourself, it is strongly recommended that you use loose-leaf albums for greater flexibility and that you incorporate subsidiary materials to illustrate the news items. Design should also be taken into account: some antiquarian examples crowd far too much on the page and the resulting flapping leaves become extremely scruffy after a few years, quite apart from the unpleasant effect on the eye. Your collection should also be indexed if its full potential is ever to be realized. Simple techniques are explained on page 29.

Prints and photographs

The collecting instinct is nowhere more evident than in the field of illustration, and the compilation of a topographical record is a contribution to the historical source material of the future. Your local history library will be a keen collector, but there is room for private individuals and local groups in this wide sphere. A group project could involve an initial exhibition in, for example, a local library, to stimulate interest in the community, the feedback being in the form of new acquisitions and material to copy. Once the historical record has been collected, the group could turn its attention to a contemporary survey through the purchase of recent postcards and a systematic photographic programme, which could perhaps be repeated at five-year intervals. In such a project one point is of the utmost importance: that the constitution of the group should make clear provision for the preservation of the records in corporate ownership, including its transfer to a suitable library or museum in the event of the group's demise. The tendency for such collections to be hoarded by individuals is pronounced, a habit which cannot but be frowned upon by historians.

The art of printed illustration began with the woodcut, which became popular on the continent from the fifteenth century. The indigenous industry dated from the beginning of the seventeenth century, by which time etched copper plates had replaced the wood blocks for the sort of work the local historian would be interested in – the topographical landscape or townscape. Some of these views were panoramic – a cross between a map and an illustration – and

Scotland boasts an early collection, the *Theatrum Scotiae*, published in 1693 by John Slezer from engraved plates drawn by the Dutchman Johannes van den Aveele and others. It was somewhat unusual in that it was published specifically as a book of illustrations: more often the prints accompanied a text of topographical description (though the reverse did occur – the text being matched to illustrations). With these books the practice developed of taking extra impressions of the prints to be sold separately. The engravings to be found in antique shops may have originated in this way, though it has also been the practice to break up volumes in order to extract the illustrations. The antique shop may also have modern copies of engravings, reproduced by the modern process of offset-litho, or even photocopying. The scrupulous dealer should make it quite clear which you are buying.

The heyday of the topographical print was the first half of the nineteenth century, Scotland being a favourite location, owing to the popularity of Sir Walter Scott's works and the taste for romantic scenery fostered by them. Scott's own *Border Antiquities* and *Provincial Antiquities and Picturesque Scenery of Scotland* were copiously illustrated, and spawned a whole series of imitations. These made use of the services of notable engravers such as W. H. Lizars, who also worked on Diddin's *Bibliographical Antiquarian and Picturesque Tour in the Northern Counties of England and in Scotland*, and Joseph Swan, publisher of volumes on Paisley, Dundee and the River Clyde. Other popular works of the period are listed in the Further Reading and Information Section of this chapter.

A note of caution is needed regarding the use of prints by the historian. The purpose of many of these collections was artistic rather than historical; indeed many plates were tampered with at each successive printing, with towers and fortifications being multiplied for dramatic effect. They are therefore not necessarily to be taken as an accurate record of the scene portrayed, a disadvantage not to be found in our next category of illustrations, the photograph, whose rapid development in the mid nineteenth century led to an equally speedy eclipse of the traditional print industry.

Some libraries hold collections of the work of outstanding pioneer photographers. Edinburgh City Library, for example, has calotypes and negatives of D. O. Hill and Robert Adamson and of Thomas Keith, while Aberdeen University Library boasts the George Washington Wilson collection. Some photographic archives have barely yet been touched by the local researcher, an example being the extension holdings of Glasgow University Archive, which include the Lind collection of several thousand negatives from the first half of the twentieth century (now indexed on computer). Two marvellous articles by George Oliver (1980) not only give an indication of the scope of such collections but are also a model for the local historian in their sensitive interpretation of the social data which they record, through the nuances of pose, composition and choice of theme.

The most widely available form of topographical photograph is the picture postcard. Encouragement was given to this form of correspondence by the introduction in 1870 of a cheap printed rate of postage. At this time the Post Office held a monopoly on postcards, as the cheap-rate stamp was engraved on the card. Permission was subsequently given to private firms to buy the official issue and print on the obverse; but as the reverse was exclusively reserved for the name and address, the picture had to be small to allow room for the message. The cards themselves were smaller too; it was not until 1899 that the Post Office allowed the larger format we are familiar with today, the extra inch making all the difference to the pictorial treatment. Two other measures contributed to the ushering in of what is known as the golden age of picture postcards, from roughly 1900 to 1918. First, in 1894 the monopoly on card production was lifted; secondly, from 1902 the address and the message could appear on the same side of the card.

During the golden age, there were three types of operation in the postcard production industry. First there were the large publishers, many of them Scottish, including W. and A. K. Johnston of Edinburgh, Millar and Lang of Glasgow, W. Ritchie and Sons of Edinburgh, George Stewart and Co., Edinburgh and Valentine and Sons Ltd, Dundee (the extensive Valentine archive is now deposited with St Andrews University). These large publishers were the only ones to survive to any extent after 1918, when the doubling of the postcard rate seriously curtailed the growth of the industry. Secondly there were small local publishers, who should not be confused with the third type – local newsagents and stationers – who appear on the cards as publishers but who in fact acted as local agents for large firms using peripatetic photographers.

In considering the enormous production of cards in this period, it must be realized that there could be up to three postal deliveries per day, the cards being used in much the same way as we would use the telephone. For the publishers the consequence was an extraordinary ferment of activity: cards recording the latest local event – a march-past of a military band, for example – could be on sale in the newsagents within a day or two. Animated street scenes, of which the latter form an example, were particularly favoured, and are of most use to the local historian in that they record social and economic activity as well as the local topography. A theme you could pursue in this respect is the holiday postcard, comparing the visual images and the messages written on the cards with the tourist guides produced by the towns concerned (your local history library will often have good collections).

Ephemera

Some attempt has been made to classify ephemera according to three main groups – the truly transient (such as the ticket), the semi-durable (the playing card, share certificate or calendar), and the keepsake (a souvenir brochure). From the collector's point of view a more useful distinction is that between contemporary and historical ephemera, the former being cheaper and easier to collect. Public libraries will be interested in both and will be able to give you names and addresses of dealers who concentrate on this field. If contemporary material appears unattractive, consider the following from Maurice Rickards (1977): 'In a decade or two – sometimes in only a year or two – we may return to it with incredulity: was that really the way things were? So much change in so short a time? These fragments, rescued, conserved, and displayed by the collector, may form a graphic social record – an encapsulated visual history.'

Printed ephemera first appeared in large quantities at the beginning of the nineteenth century. There are so many possible themes to pursue that they cannot be dealt with individually here, but two examples can suffice to give a flavour of the subject.

Tradesmen's cards date from the seventeenth century and were all-purpose items – advertisements, jotters and posters – engraved with the name of the tradesman concerned and packed with information. They were designed to catch the eyes of the gentry who alone were rich enough to afford their services, and to this end devices such as coats of arms, flourishes and obsequious language were used. The trade card was the ancestor of all printed business material, including bills, letterheads and brochures. A particularly interesting development was the pictorial representation of the business premises within a design of elaborate scrollwork, noticeable in the 1870s and attributed to the influence of Art Nouveau styles. For a reason which you might want to investigate, it remained a strong influence on business stationery design up to the 1940s, by which time it represented a curious anomaly. Printing techniques and influences can become a subject of study in their own right. Price lists and advertising leaflets appear at the start of the nineteenth century, and unlike the trade cards which were engraved they were produced by jobbing printers. Newspaper advertisements begin at this time too and can be used in conjunction with business ephemera to construct, for example, the history of the shops in a street. Trade directories will afford supplementary information.

A second example is the illustration of a town's history through its ephemera. A good collection might include bills announcing the ending of hostilities or victory celebrations, election leaflets, satirical broadsheets, public notices, civic week programmes and menus from council banquets. As a possible project, consider the idea of collecting all the contemporary ephemera of your town within a limited period. The result could be a marvellous picture of your community frozen in time – a source of fascination to future inhabitants and local historians.

Organizing your collection should be an important priority once the considerations of physical condition and storage of the items have been dealt with. The first task is to make an inventory, either on archival principles (see pp. 33–4) or more simply at random according to a running number (for identification) with a brief description of each item's form (poster, programme, etc.), the body responsible for its publication (publisher, not printer) and its content. The second stage, which is even more important, is to index the collection, preferably on 13 cm × 8 cm cards. The main criterion of a good index (particularly if it is to grow to any size) is consistency. There are two aspects, the linguistic and the analytical. Linguistic consistency involves the elimination of synonyms and different forms (i.e. use 'mills' and 'breweries' or 'milling' and 'brewing', but not 'breweries' and 'milling'). Analytical consistency is achieved by using indexing categories, any subject lending itself to being broken down into people (names of individuals or groups), institutions, objects (physical or mental), activities or events (brewing, fishing, etc.), places and times. You will not necessarily want or be able to use all categories for every item, but together they comprise every possible aspect of a subject. The chosen heading is placed at the top of each card and items which relate to it can be listed underneath by their identification number (this saves the work of copying out the details under every subject heading). If you so wish, categories can be combined to give composite headings – 'symphony concert', for example, or 'coal mining' – both of which combine 'object' with 'activity'. In using composite headings consistency is once again important – if the order in which you combine is 'object:activity', you must observe this rule on every occasion and not use headings such as concert, jazz (activity:object). If you want a really detailed index, you can combine whole strings of categories, again in a set order, as follows: symphony concert: town hall: 1984 (object: activity:place:time). You might wonder why you cannot make entries under all possible permutations: the answer is that your index would soon run to millions of items. One solution, if you have the technical knowledge, is to hold your index on a home computer, which is admirably suited to the purpose. Each category can be tagged with its own code and you can then interrogate the files with questions such as 'What do I have relating to the town hall?' or 'What records tell me about life in 1984?'.

The local historian should not underestimate the value of indexes. He will encounter them in the local history library, where they serve two purposes: to allow quick access to specific pieces of information (in the same way that an index at the back of a book provides access to the contents of the book) and to juxtapose evidence from different sources, whose interrelationship may often be unexpected and supply the catalyst for an original piece of research. By an extension of this idea, the local historian himself can generate unsuspected and illuminating connections by applying indexing techniques to the sources he is using: in Chapter Four an example of this approach is developed in the context of an anthropological study of a community.

One final point in connection with collections of any kind concerns provision for their future. If you have spent a lot of effort in compilation, you should make arrangements for a local museum or library or record office to inherit on your death.

Bibliographies

It is not absolutely necessary for you to consult bibliographies: you can avoid them, first, by getting the library staff to do all the work for you, though there are disadvantages to this. They may not have time to make a comprehensive search, particularly among specialized materials such as journal articles and university theses; and the study of bibliographies may itself suggest new lines of enquiry which a searcher working on your behalf will not be in a position to appreciate. A second possible strategy is to use the bibliographical references given in the first book you read to introduce you to the next, and so on. There are two shortcomings here: if the first book you read was published ten years ago, you will never find out about material published since; and the subject you are researching is unlikely to match exactly the books you are reading. For best results, a combination of all three options is recommended.

A bibliography is a list of books or similar materials. It differs from a catalogue only in that a catalogue is a list of books belonging to a particular institution; a bibliography is a list on a particular subject or relating to a particular locality. It can be seen therefore that the catalogue of a local history library *is* a bibliography, and in most cases it will be the best and most up-to-date one for your area. It will not be comprehensive (the library may not have been able to acquire some rare or expensive items) but it will be continually updated, which is not the case with published bibliographies. The latter are of value, however, especially in the detailed information they sometimes give about obscure articles which form part of national archives. Your local history library will have copies of any referring to your locality, and a complete list (some are up to 100 years old) appears in Norma E. S. Armstrong, *Local Collections in Scotland*, SLA, 1977. As well as local bibliographies, you may also want to consult those concerned with your subject. Areas that are well covered include Scottish education and economic history, relevant titles being listed in the Further Reading and Information sections of this book.

General Scottish bibliographies will list material by both subject and place. For the subject search, they can be used to find out what has been written in the national context; for the local search they can help to provide information about titles published after the date of your local bibliography (if indeed one exists for your area). Of the Scottish bibliographies, there are two which are regarded as the standard texts, namely Arthur Mitchell and Caleb George Cash, *A Contribution to the Bibliography of Scottish Topography*, Constable, 1917 (2 volumes) and its successor, Philip David Hancock, *A Bibliography of Works Relating to Scotland 1916–50*, Edinburgh University Press, 1959–60 (2 volumes). Between 1950 and 1976 there is unfortunately a gap in the general coverage of Scottish books, filled in part only by *Reader's Guide to Scotland: a Bibliography*, National Book League, 1968. For the rest, recourse must be had to the *British National Bibliography* (annual since 1950), a complete list of all books published in the United Kingdom; this has the advantage of being indexed in considerable depth under both subject and place. It is more complicated to use, being based on the Dewey Decimal Classification, and you will perhaps want library staff to advise you. Since 1976–7 the *Bibliography of Scotland* has been produced annually by the National Library of Scotland. It is by far the most detailed bibliography to have appeared, and is not limited to books, but includes journal articles, reports and so on. Like the two traditional bibliographies of Scotland, it is arranged in two sections – place and subject – though the headings used are much more detailed and specific. Journal articles are an important source of information and should certainly not be neglected. Good coverage is to be found in the annual bibliography that appears in the journal *Scottish Historical Review*, which incidentally does cover books as well, and can be used for the difficult period 1950–76. The *British Humanities Index* is an annual devoted exclusively to journal articles. Nineteenth-century articles, which can often be used as primary source material (topographical accounts for example or guides to great mansion houses) are listed in *The Wellesley Index to Victorian Periodicals 1824–1900*.

Other libraries

The study of published records may require visits to other libraries. The cities of Aberdeen, Dundee, Edinburgh and Glasgow maintain large collections of Scottish reference materials which will not be found in rural library authorities' holdings. You may also want to go to the National Library of Scotland, George IV Bridge, Edinburgh EH1 1EW, which is one of Britain's half dozen copyright libraries, receiving by right a copy of every book published in the country. The Department of Printed Books holds rare and valuable items and early royal commission reports which may not be obtainable elsewhere. None of the material is available for loan. It is preferable to take along with you means of identification. To use a university library (unless you are a past or present member of the university) will require special permission, which should be sought in writing before your visit. University libraries have strong collections in periodicals, and are also the main source for university theses, an important and neglected secondary source for local historians. Theses however can usually be borrowed for you by your local library. They are listed in *Aslib Index to Theses Accepted for Higher Degrees by the Universities of Great Britain and Ireland* (annual since 1950–51; latterly bi-annual). Retrospective searching is by means of R. R. Bilboul and F. L. Kent, *Retrospective Index to Theses of Great Britain and Ireland 1716–1950*, ABC–Clio, 1975.

The foregoing survey of the public library will hopefully have given you an idea of the scope of its collections. If, for the reasons discussed earlier, you intend to restrict your studies to this source, you will want to look carefully at the kinds of project outlined in the preceding pages. The challenge is considerable, but there are tricks that can be employed. One example has already been touched on: though a distinction has been made between primary and secondary sources, we have also seen that many secondary sources are also primary sources if observed from an oblique angle. Following this train of thought, you can discover that almost anything can be a primary source. In a study of local printing methods, for example, nearly the whole of the local history library becomes a primary source, as it does for a project investigating how local history studies have developed in your area. In general terms, projects based upon the comparison of sources rather than the extraction of data from them will be well suited to a library-based study. One such project might be to compare the news coverage of two local newspapers in relation to the political stance of the editors or proprietors.

Chapters Four to Six of this book outline specific themes, some of which could be explored through library-based projects (guidance is given in each case as to what records are likely to be held by local history libraries). Other projects could be suitably adapted – it is essential to rid oneself of the idea that research demands a complete survey of the available material. As long as findings are expressed in terms of the materials used, the conclusions reached can be quite valid.

The next chapter is devoted to a consideration of record offices and archives. Whether you can become a regular user will likely depend, as will be explained, on which part of Scotland you inhabit. In some areas you may have a record office virtually on your doorstep (it may in fact be administered by your local history library); in others, for example the Highlands, you must resign yourself to being unable to make regular use, though there are today fewer and fewer regions where this is the case. But if you cannot use a record office, it does not mean that the work you do will be of less value. The essential quality of historical study is not the material used, but the imaginative exploitation of what is available.

Chapter Three

ARCHIVE OFFICES AND THEIR RECORDS

An archive has been defined as 'all documents . . . accumulated and preserved by a natural process in the course of the conduct of affairs of any kind, public or private, at any date, and surviving in the keeping of the persons responsible for the business or their successors'. The reference to documents rather than institutions is important. However, popular speech (and even the names of institutions themselves) tends to blur the distinction, and references are made to archives in circumstances in which 'archive office' is the technically correct term. With the definition in mind, we can also establish a clear difference between a library and an archive, in that a library is a collection of material (traditionally books, but, as we have seen, including many other types of record) from various origins and brought together for convenience of study. An archive, on the other hand, is a collection of material from a single source preserved in its integrity. The consequences in respect of the different organization of library collections and archives are quite profound. It is essential that the conceptual distinction be grasped, for it transcends the institutions concerned – libraries for example can and do hold archives as well as their other collections, but will organize them according to an archivist's, not a librarian's, principles.

On a superficial level you will notice that whereas in most cases you can browse among library collections, you will rarely be able to do so among archives. The documents will be brought to you, immediate access being given only to inventories, whose organization and function must therefore be clearly understood. More importantly, given that the provenance of an archive is of the utmost significance, constraints are imposed upon its possible arrangement, even though it may consist of disparate material both in form (maps, charters, ledgers, diaries, books and bus tickets) and in subject (an estate's papers for example may contain household account books, rentals, plans for the rebuilding of the mansion house and notes on crop rotation experiments). Despite the most extreme diversity, however, the archive must be preserved as a unit, whereas a librarian, who is free to place items wherever they may be of greatest value to the user, arranges his material according to various subjects and/or localities, with broad areas divided into more specific ones. In addition a librarian will catalogue each item under the person or body responsible for its content, thereby producing one alphabetical listing of all material held. An archive, on the other hand, must be arranged according to the internal logic of the records themselves, reflecting the administrative or legal structure of the institution and its historical development. It is certainly not combined with similar material from other archives. Instead of a catalogue, *inventories* (or preliminary *handlists*) are compiled, which list all the items within an archive according to this logical arrangement. The librarian will allocate to each item a class number – a different number for each subject – which is reproduced in the order of the books on the shelves; the archivist will give items a code number, consisting of a general code for the type of institutions (for example B for a burgh, CO for a county council and so on), an identification number for a specific institution within the type, and a further number to identify the separate items in the institution's archive. Each document is thereby uniquely identified.

For the researcher interested in a particular subject or place rather than an institution, the archival arrangement is not of the greatest value, but there are two ways in which the archivist attempts to alleviate the problems caused by the necessary limitation on his freedom. Though he cannot meddle with the archives, he can manipulate duplicate copies of inventories, to produce thematic source lists on a variety of subjects. Relevant source lists produced by the Scottish Record Office will be mentioned at appropriate points in the text (these are not published lists). A second course of action open to the archivist is to compile detailed indexes (under name, place and subject) to the contents of documents. However, one is not going to find vast numbers of documents indexed in this way, demanding as it does considerable outlays of effort, with the exception of those records, such as registers, where indexing is a fundamental function of the original compilation.

Archives can be broadly divided into four categories: *central government*, *church*, *private* and *local government*. Those of central government and the established church (Church of Scotland) are almost exclusively deposited in the Scottish Record Office. Considerable collections of private papers are held there too, but many other institutions boast holdings in this field, including the National Library of Scotland Department of Manuscripts, university libraries, museums, and regional and district archive offices. Collections still in private hands are numerous (for example family papers of landed gentry and aristocracy, business records and solicitors' files) but a systematic national survey of these archives has been conducted, the data being recorded with the National Register of Archives for Scotland. The register is maintained by the Scottish Record Office and a phone call or letter is sufficient to confirm the existence, location and content of any archive (held publicly or privately).

In the case of local government records, we find no regular pattern of deposit, partly because recent trends towards decentralization have yet to reach a definite conclusion. Had this passage been written twenty years ago, one could confidently have said that local government records were either retained as working collections in the hands of the authorities concerned, or had been deposited in the Scottish Record Office. The latter's traditional dominance in the holding of local records appears to have been the result of accident rather than design, and was certainly not the ideal propounded by some of the outstanding early keepers. This has been recognized, and the Scottish Record Office now encourages the formation, under suitable supervision, of local archive offices, a process facilitated by the establishment of larger local government authorities in 1974 to replace the previous fragmented system. The new Scottish regional councils have reacted in different ways: some have set up regional archive offices (Strathclyde, Grampian, Central); others have provided, either as an alternative or in conjunction with these, district archive offices, which may also be established by the district councils (often the library service); in others no development has taken place. The final pattern has still not crystallized.

Given the different origins of the local offices, it is not possible to generalize about their holdings: some have had extensive collections passed to them from the Scottish Record Office, others little or nothing. However, the core archives will usually be those of the old county councils and town councils, together with the records of their predecessors (commissioners of supply, justices of the peace, lieutenants, road trustees, etc.). In addition church records (kirk session and presbytery), which at one time were exclusively held by the Scottish Record Office, have been devolved, with the approval of local presbyteries. In the case of Orkney and Shetland, sheriff court records have been transferred, which may set a precedent. Relevant private family and estate papers will consist both of new deposits, for which the local office has been suggested as the most appropriate home, and devolved Scottish Record Office archives. A complete list of transmitted records appears in the *Annual Report of the Keeper of the Records of Scotland for 1982* (with further items mentioned in the 1983 report), and the Scottish Record Office now maintains a register of current locations of local authority files. In all cases where holdings have been relinquished, microfilm copies are retained for security and for use by centrally situated researchers. Local archive offices established to date are listed in the Further Reading and Information section of this chapter, though you will also be able to find out the current position regarding your area through your local history library.

The local record office is a new venture which deserves all the support it can get from the local historian, for whom, after all, it is primarily intended. Generalizations about layout and regulations are impossible to make, but it will be modelled basically on the pattern of the Scottish Record Office. It will be easier to use, however, in that there will be fewer archives and they will all be relevant to your local studies. Given the choice, you should find its use preferable, even if a visit to Edinburgh presents no problem for you.

The Scottish Record Office

The Scottish Record Office remains the single most important institution in respect of both public and private archives. The main building is at the east end of Princes Street, Edinburgh, opposite the Post Office and fronted by an equestrian statue of Wellington. For correspondence, write to The Keeper of the Records of Scotland, PO Box 36, HM General Register House, Edinburgh EH1 3YY (telephone 031 556 6585). When you enter, ask at the enquiry desk in the foyer to be directed to the Historical Search Room. You will need to leave your coat and baggage and will be shown the way, which incidentally will take you through the Legal Search Room used primarily by the legal profession. As you enter the Historical Search Room, the enquiry desk will be facing you: the staff here are not specialist advisers – their job is to ensure conformity to regulations and to fetch for you the documents you require. You will first need to apply there for a reader's ticket (renewable annually); it will be issued to you by the advisory staff who occupy a separate room to the right. Regulations will be explained to you – the most important relate to the care of documents (which obviously must not be handled roughly or piled up in ungainly heaps). Another rule requires all note-taking to be in pencil, so you will need to be suitably equipped. Pencils become blunt surprisingly quickly, and one is not encouraged to sharpen pencils at the desks. The advisory staff will also be able to give you advice on how to pursue your project, though they obviously will not have the time to explain in detail all the possible ramifications.

To help you in that task you can turn to the finding aids, indexes and written guides that are located in the ante-room between the Historical Search Room and the advisers' office. It is here that you should spend your first hour in the Scottish Record Office, beginning with the *inventories*, which are kept in alphabetical order by code. Thus burgh records (B) will precede Scottish Education Department records (ED) and so on. Take your time to browse through relevant inventories; indeed, if it be possible, you can save time by consulting them beforehand (inventories of local government records at least are likely to be held by your local history library). If not, study relevant sections in detail and also look for the valuable *prefaces* written by specialist members of staff. The selection of items you require to see is made from the inventories, the full code number being copied on to slips together with your desk number and passed to the staff at the main enquiry desk. A maximum of three items is allowed at one time, so you are advised to plan your day carefully. Also in the ante-room are kept the *source lists* together with relevant books and articles on the records and their use. A third group of aids are the *indexes to registers* and, depending on the nature of your project, they can be of great value in their own right, without your necessarily having recourse to the documents to which they relate. Their use will be examined in later chapters. In the Historical Search Room itself are displayed the major series of published Scottish records, together with reference books.

Expansion of Scottish Record Office collections has necessitated the purchase of a second building in Charlotte Square, which is known as West Register House (the search room upstairs is called the West Search Room). Held here are maps and plans, papers of the nationalized industries and company records, amongst others, together with duplicate sets of inventories.

The standard guide to the holdings of the Scottish Record Office is M. Livingstone, *Guide to the Public Records of Scotland*, HMSO, 1905, to which a supplement appeared in the *Scottish Historical Review*, volume 26, no. 101, April 1947. For subsequent accessions, a list is given in the *Annual Reports of the Keeper Of the Records* and the October issues of *Scottish Historical Review*. A new guide to the records is in preparation, and draft copies can be consulted in the historical search rooms. For preliminary study, a series of leaflets is provided free of charge (they are listed in the Further Reading and Information section of this chapter); particularly recommended is *Leaflet No. 7*, which contains a concise outline of the holdings. Published material from Scottish Record Office archives is listed in *British National Archives* (Government Publications Sectional List 24), which is periodically updated. As already mentioned, it would be foolish to waste valuable time studying documents which you could read at leisure in your own home or library in a published version.

Other record offices

The National Library of Scotland has already been referred to in connection with its Department of Printed Books. There are however two other major departments, both of which are concerned with primary sources. One is the Map Room, situated at 137 Causewayside, Edinburgh EH9 1PH, which is eventually to share premises with the Science Reference Library currently under construction on the site. The other is the Department of Manuscripts, which shares the George IV Bridge building. The core of this collection was inherited from the older Advocates' Library (dating from 1680), a catalogue of whose material has been published as the *Summary Catalogue of Advocates Manuscripts*. Development has occurred, not least in a literary and political direction, but for our purposes the most important records are estate and business papers, of which there has been a policy of systematic acquisition. Trade union records are also strongly represented. Printed catalogues of holdings fill five published volumes (many others remain unpublished).

Two major collections of thematic significance are the responsibility of specialized institutions: the General Register Office (next door to the Scottish Record Office) holds current and former registers of births, marriages and deaths and census data, which, concerning the individual as they do, are more appropriately considered in the next chapter; and similarly the chapter on buildings is the suitable place to discuss the National Monuments Record. Other specialized collections are also treated in context. They include those of the School of Scottish Studies (oral records), the Scottish Catholic Archives, the Property Services Agency (photographs) and health board archives. University archive collections are by no means confined to the records of the universities themselves. Glasgow shipbuilding records, for example, form part of Glasgow University Archives, and local government records for North East Fife are deposited with St Andrews University Archives. The specialized Scottish Brewing Archive is part of Heriot-Watt University. The Scottish Record Office's strategy is to strengthen these regional collections by appropriate transfers and deposits.

Museums are sometimes neglected as sources of primary material – represented both by the artefacts which they display and by supporting documentation. In 1985 the two major national museums, the National Museum of Antiquities of Scotland, Queen Street, Edinburgh EH2 1JD (with strong collections in archaeology and farming life), and the Royal Scottish Museum, Chambers Street, Edinburgh EH1 1JF were amalgamated. Traditional local museums have been joined in recent years by others based on themes, such as fishing and coal mining. Information about museum collections can be found in two annual publications, *Museums and Galleries in Great Britain and Ireland* and *Museums and Galleries in Scotland*. Use of pictorial sources in local history research is facilitated by the *Social History Index* compiled and maintained by the Scottish Portrait Gallery.

Using archives

Written records are the historian's stock-in-trade, and one or two preliminary remarks on their use are appropriate. The first is a repetition of a point already made – that handwriting before 1700 is impossible to read without prior training, either through organized courses or a study of the literature or the subject. Preparatory work should also extend to background research into the period and records in question: it is best not to tackle archives at the outset of your project. Thirdly, it is strongly recommended that you try to acquire a general grounding in Scots law. For the use of registers, the knowledge is indispensable, but for many other records – company papers, charters, leases, court actions – it can dramatically increase the understanding of the documents being considered. If there is one factor that can turn an indifferent local historian into an accomplished one, it is the insight and confidence provided by a grasp of legal ideas.

A final point is the desirability of adopting a critical attitude towards archives, in much the same way as one would, say, towards an article in a popular newspaper. In the latter case one is aware of the possible political bias of the writer and his capacity for misrepresentation, but an official record is no less subject to distortion. The researcher must always be looking for independent corroborations and for the establishment of a broader context that will allow him to see the predisposition of the men and institutions he is dealing with, and indeed he must actively seek to present alternative viewpoints, where possible, in the pursuit of these aims. To accept the outlook of any class or group affects the historian's freedom of judgement, and he is the poorer for it.

As well as avoiding timorousness in the face of records, the researcher should also try not to be overawed by the record offices, however vast and grand they may seem. One need not be ashamed of one's ignorance, for very few people are expert in more than a small area. Indeed, it is the mark of the true scholar that he neither despises those who do not know, nor admits to knowing much himself. The staff you meet in the record offices will be wanting to help you as much as they can – it is after all their job, and their pride in their profession will demand it.

The decision as to what records to use for a project needs careful thought: it is not sufficient that they are known to relate to your locality. You must know what kind of information they contain, and even more important, what kind of use can be made of it. Once you have consulted the inventories in some detail, it is suggested that you, as it were, make a few test bores, asking to see samples of different types of material, using them to try out some questions that may be germinating in your mind. If they prove unhelpful, are there other records which might be better? Or is it that your questions are not being well formulated? Whatever the case the one thing you must not do is to pick on an archive and start copying down extracts at random. You will either become bored after a few pages and give up or, if you persist, will end up with an extensive collection of miscellaneous and unusable bric-à-brac. It is not the function of the historian to create a duplicate archive of his locality like a squirrel's hoard of nuts. The records are quite safe where they are – what they need is an interpreter.

The remainder of this chapter is devoted to the sort of examination of written records which will hopefully enable you to conduct your test bores with more confidence and likelihood of success. Thumbnail sketches are provided of the origins, contents, value and accessibility of different archives – all of which factors need to be taken into account when making your choice.

Central government records

The use of national records by the local historian needs some justification; there are three main arguments in its favour. First, they can give the general context, though in some respects (particularly in connection with parliamentary legislative papers both before and after the Union) the standard secondary sources are often a quicker and more efficient means of establishing the national framework. Secondly, Scotland has always been a small nation in terms of population (smaller than London); thus its records can refer to very localized projects and events. Scottish Office departmental files and royal commission reports are examples. The third argument is an extension of the second: in its judicial capacity the state interacts directly with the individual or local institution. Certain types of civil and criminal action have always been the exclusive preserve of central courts, which also serve as courts of appeal from the lower courts.

Substantial parts of the administrative and executive records of the Scottish state have been published, including the *Acts of the Parliament of Scotland 1124–1707* (12 volumes) and the *Register of the Privy Council of Scotland 1545–1691* (over 30 volumes; publication still in progress), which contains both its *acta* (administrative acts) and its *decreets* (judicial decisions) together with a number of other documents (warrants, bonds, proclamations, etc.). The Privy Council, established in 1489, was a committee of advisers selected to pursue the day-to-day administration of the country – economic development, roads and bridges, crime control and poor relief. *The Calendar of Documents relating to Scotland 1108–1509* (four volumes) is a miscellaneous collection of material that has found its way into the Public Record Office in London. All the above are HMSO or Register House publications.

Legislation of the British Parliament affecting Scotland has been collected together in the *Public General Statutes affecting Scotland 1707–1847*, HMSO, 1848 (three volumes); annual volumes of the same title cover later years. Of greater interest will be local acts of Parliament, which are concerned with specific projects such as a harbour, tramway or road. They are listed in *Index to Local and Personal Acts 1801–1947*, HMSO, 1949, to which a supplementary index for the years 1948–66 was published in 1967. The work is kept up to date through the tables and indexes of the annual volumes of

Local and Personal Acts. Your local history library will probably hold or have access to most of the local acts affecting your area; if you are lucky, they will also have files of submissions made by interested parties supporting or opposing the bill.

Of even greater value to the local historian are royal commission reports. The remit of the commissions was to examine topics of public concern and to make recommendations for legislation. They are of course still part of our parliamentary system today but they were particularly significant in the nineteenth century when industrialization put considerable strains on the existing administrative framework. The popular name for them was 'blue books'. Less prestigious but still of value are the departmental committees set up by specific state ministries for a similar purpose. A good bibliography of the subject is by W. R. Purcell, *Local History from Blue Books*, Routledge & Kegan Paul, 1962. A broad range of economic, social and industrial issues to be found in other parliamentary papers is the subject of bibliographies by Percy and Grace Ford and successors, listed in the Further Reading and Information section of this chapter. Government publications are complex and varied: a useful up-to-date guide is David Butcher, *Official Publications in Britain*, Bingley, 1983.

Scottish Record Office Exchequer records (E) contain many riches for the local historian. The remodelled Exchequer, post-1707, was responsible for administering what are known as Forfeited Estates, from which a fascinating series of papers has survived. Major Scottish estates, especially in the Highlands, were forfeited to the crown after both Jacobite rebellions (1715 and 1745). The records of the administration of the 1745 Forfeited Estates are particularly rich, giving a detailed picture of daily life. Most were eventually sold by public auction. Published extracts and summaries include *Scottish Forfeited Estate Papers 1715:1745*, Scottish History Society, 1909; *Statistics of the Annexed Estates 1755–56*, HMSO, 1973; and *Reports on the Annexed Estates, 1755–69*, HMSO, 1973. Rentals for 1721 and 1726 have also been published in extracts by the Scottish History Society. You are advised to check whether any estates in which you are interested are included in this category.

The Union of 1707 contained no reference to the machinery of central government, a shortcoming which was to lead to piecemeal development of institutions in response to specific needs, with periods of neglect following on the heels of uninformed interference. Bodies that were instituted include the Scottish Excise Board (1707); the Board of Manufactures (1727), whose records chart Scotland's industrial growth in the eighteenth century, mainly in textiles (it has an odd inventory code – NG – a result of the transfer of its remaining assets to the National Galleries in the nineteenth century); the Fishery Board (1809); the General Board of Directors of Prisons (1839); and the Board of Supervision for Relief of the Poor (1845).

Some of these boards later evolved to form departments of the Scottish Office. The Scottish Privy Council was abolished in 1708 and overall responsibility for Scottish affairs was transferred to one of the London-based secretaries of state and later to the home secretary, the latter being assisted by the lord advocate as the resident official in Scotland.

The most significant development in the modern period was the creation of the office of secretary for Scotland in 1885. The post took over responsibility for the various boards, together with those aspects of Scottish affairs formerly the province of the home secretary. In 1928 statutory departments for agriculture and health were set up, and in 1939 more substantial powers were devolved, the departments being organized under the umbrella of the Scottish Office. Departmental files are transferred to the Scottish Record Office after thirty years in most cases, and the records of the various boards of earlier periods are engrossed with those of the departments which succeeded them. Thus the Fishery Board papers are with those of the Department of Agriculture, Fisheries and Food.

Scottish Education Department archives (code ED) include school inspection reports from 1847. These used to be confidential under the thirty years rule but are now published as the reports are made. The Scottish Home and Health Department was formerly two departments – the Home Department and the Health Department. It carries out many of the duties fulfilled by the Home Office in England and Wales in respect of police, fire services and the administration of courts. Its remit in health matters includes supervision of the National Health Service in Scotland and of the 15 health boards. Former functions in the provision of sanitation, water supply and housing are now performed by the Scottish Development Department (DD), which is also responsible for transport planning and communications. Home and Health files (HH) include the nineteenth-century prison board records, prison registers from as early as 1657, Board of Supervision papers (dealing with poor law administration and public health in the nineteenth century), hospital archives from the late eighteenth century and police records from 1887. The Scottish Economic Planning Department (SEP), established in 1973, has deposited files on Highland development from 1936, new towns from 1910 and electricity from 1943. The Department of Agriculture, Fisheries and Food's records (AF) include harbour plans, a valuable series of agricultural censuses for each parish since 1866 and crofting papers 1866–1940.

As well as the departments of the Scottish Office, the secretary of state for Scotland is responsible for various aspects of the work of United Kingdom departments in so far as they relate to Scottish affairs. The corresponding records, also held in the Scottish Record Office, include the papers of dissolved limited liability companies (Department of Trade – BT), territorial and auxiliary archives

(Ministry of Defence – MD) and files on ancient monuments, parks and public buildings (Department of the Environment – MW). Similarly the Scottish Record Office is the repository for records of the nationalized industries in their Scottish operations. Archives of companies taken over by the state at nationalization are included: thus British Rail records (BR) contain railway company papers from 1807, the National Coal Board (CB) those of coal companies from 1741 and the Scottish Gas Board (GB) those of local gas enterprises from the early nineteenth century.

The Scottish Record Office plans to publish a guide to its departmental records. A draft copy can be consulted in the West Search Room.

Judicial records

Judicial records, both civil and criminal, are a fascinating source for the local historian. As Peter Worsley (1970) states: 'The sociological imagination . . . consists in the ability to appreciate that the "troubles" that afflict the individual are the outcome of much wider arrangements within which his life is lived out and that these arrangements affect the local family and work milieu . . .' In other words, human beings in extremities of fear, humiliation, hatred, anger and despair can reveal more of themselves and the society in which they live than the official versions of history, which often have as one of their functions the maintenance of the seemingly smooth operation of a society. Conflict reveals the cracks in the smooth surface, and gives us a glimpse of the caverns below. Criminal records in particular demonstrate the existence of sub-cultures, with standards and goals quite different from the established consensus, which itself may only be that established by historians who have based their judgement on the partial evidence of the official accounts of the time. Most individuals do not participate in the construction of an era's recorded view of itself, and court records afford an opportunity to investigate their viewpoint.

Examples of just two types of action in the Court of Session will give an indication of the potential of these archives. *Cessio bonorum* processes represented a distinct category within creditor/debtor law. Before the establishment of modern bankruptcy law through the procedure of sequestration, debtors were at the mercy of their creditors, who could have them imprisoned, in which predicament they were even less in a position to find the wherewithal to honour their debts. By the device of *Cessio bonorum* however they could surrender their estate to their creditors and go free without further impediment. They had to prove before the court that there were mitigating circumstances that might excuse their situation, and the detailed arguments that were put forward give a unique insight into social and economic conditions as seen from the individual's point of view. The second example concerns actions for defamation, in which we can witness the unusual spectacle of a community 'washing its dirty linen' in public: unspoken feelings are expressed which may subsequently be regretted by the parties concerned and their witnesses – but not by the local historian.

The central courts make a clear distinction between civil and criminal jurisdiction. The first is associated with the Court of Session, and the second with the High Court of Justiciary and its circuit courts. In its present form the Court of Session dates from 1532, though its origin is earlier, in the meeting of representatives from the three estates of parliament (that is, the clergy, barons and commissioners of burghs) to serve as a judicial body (separation of executive and judiciary was an English phenomenon only). Fixed sittings were held – thus the word 'session'.

It is useful to be aware of some of the terminology of civil actions, also known as *causes*. A *process* refers to the collection of papers relating to an action, which commences when a *summons* is served by one party on another and a copy lodged with the court. It includes a statement of the case of the *pursuer* which is called the *condescendence*. In turn the *defender* has a chance to put forward his version of the facts; and each in turn can modify and develop his arguments in response to what the other has submitted. Whilst this procedure is in train, the papers are described as an *open record*; when finished, as a *closed record*. If the facts are in dispute, the case is heard before a jury; if an interpretation of law solely, before a judge alone. In either case, the successful party is issued with an *extract*, an official copy of the decision of the court, of which a duplicate becomes part of the Register of Acts and Decreets. The extracted process constitutes a *warrant* – the sanction for the successful party to have the court's decision implemented. As well as actions, the object of which is to 'enforce a legal right against a defender who resists it, or to protect a legal right which the defender is infringing', the Court of Session also deals with *petitions*, the purpose of which is generally to obtain from the court approval for a course of action. In such cases, the parties are not usually in dispute. Included in this category are sequestrations, liquidation of companies and changes in the administration of trusts.

Court of Session archives (CS) date from 1478 and are somewhat complex to use, partly through deficiencies of indexing. They include the following.

1. *Minute Books of the Registers of Acts and Decreets* kept by the clerks of the court, with brief notes on the nature of the actions and the names of parties. The first series covers the years 1557–1659 and is fairly comprehensive from 1576. The second series continues the record to the early nineteenth century, and the third is the current series. The Minute Books were first printed in 1782, since which time they have been issued in annual volumes. For some periods,

they constitute the only indexed facility for the researcher.
2. *Registers of Acts and Decreets*, in which the decisions of the court are recorded. The first series covers 1542–1659; the second 1661–1810; the third 1810–21; the fourth 1821–9; and the fifth is the current series. Up to 1810 the court operated with three clerks' offices: the unfortunate result is that there are three separate registers to consult, under the names of the three offices, Dalrymple, Durie and Mackenzie. The first series has however been placed in a combined order and numbered consecutively. The same problem of parallel series applies also to other Court of Session records. Some of the early Registers of Acts and Decreets have been published: these include the *Acts of the Lords Auditors of Causes and Complaints 1466–1501*, the *Acts of the Lords of Council in Public Affairs 1501–1544* (a selection only, dealing with administrative rather than legal matters) and the *Acts of the Lords of Council in Civil Causes 1478–1503*, all of which concern the period when the Court of Session, Privy Council and other bodies were not entirely differentiated. The later Acts and Decreets have not been published, and up to 1810 have not been indexed, except for parts of the collection held by the Signet Library. From 1810 there has been an annual index. The Register of Acts and Decreets became at one stage a virtual transcript of all the papers in an action, but this practice was discontinued at the start of the nineteenth century.
3. *Register of Deeds*, which is discussed in Chapter Six.
4. *Extracted and Unextracted Processes*, which are the claims and counter-claims lodged with the court by pursuer and defender. Unextracted processes are those actions withdrawn before judgment was made: some were abandoned, others put to arbitration to save costs. The Scottish Record Office is currently engaged in an indexing programme. Bill Chamber processes emanate from a distinct court within the Court of Session for diligence (see pp. 130–1) and bankruptcy, their use being facilitated by the *Index to Bill Chamber Processes 1670–1882*.
5. *Productions*, which are any documents or artefacts lodged with the court as part of evidence. They may be 'anything from a thimble to a traction engine or a scrap of paper to a probative document'. A list of productions is being prepared for publication by the Scottish Record Office.

A report on all the Court of Session records appears in the *Annual Report of the Keeper of the Records of Scotland for 1972*.

It will be apparent that the Court of Session has generated a large number of papers, many of which are published in duplicate (the pleadings for example) and reproduced at different stages of the legal process. After the Union further sets were produced when the practice arose of allowing appeal from the Court of Session to the House of Lords, where an uneasy relationship subsisted between the very different English and Scottish legal systems. There are therefore other collections, notably those in the Signet Library, which is not generally open to the public, though arrangements can be made in the case of serious researchers. There are two advantages in using the Signet Library: first, since the introduction of the annual *Session Cases* (see below) in 1821 its holdings have been organized to correspond with the reported cases, thus providing quicker access to the documents required: secondly, parts of the collection have been indexed, both under names and subjects (for eighteenth-century records in particular, the index is the best finding-aid available).

As has been said before, the amateur historian should as far as possible make use of public library materials, a stricture which applies nowhere more forcibly than to the complex Court of Session papers. The researcher who arrives at the Scottish Record Office wanting to look through the court records relating to his area is wasting his time: he is trying to do more than is possible for a professional, let alone an amateur. What would be feasible, if he were making a detailed study of a locality during a short period of time, would be to consult the Minute Books of that era, but for researches of any more extensive scope the following strategy is recommended.

First, check your local published bibliography – some do include indexes of relevant cases. Secondly you may find references in parish and family histories and in newspaper articles. Thirdly, consult the legal profession's published reports, which are to be found on the shelves of the larger reference libraries. These, though they do not provide the detail to be found in the process papers, should be used at the very least for ascertaining the dates and substance of relevant actions. There are two sources for pre-eighteenth-century records. One is the volumes of *Practicks* – notes made by private individuals or judges and subsequently published; the other is the collections of decisions, again often compiled by judges, and annotated with their comments and interpretations. An official reporter was appointed only in 1705 and from 1752 to 1841 his reports were published in *Faculty Decisions*. The eighteenth century and earlier periods are also covered by Henry Home Kames and A. F. Tytler, *The Decisions of the Court of Session*, volumes 1 and 2, Bell & Bradfute, 1791, volumes 3 and 4, William Creech, 1797 (covering 1540–1796) and William Maxwell Morison, *Decisions of the Court of Session*, Bell & Bradfute, 1801–7; and by Tait, 1826 (26 volumes up to 1826) to which there is a published index, *Index to the Decisions of the Court of Session Contained in all the Original Collections and in Mr Morison's Dictionary of Decisions*, Court of Session, 1823. From 1821 there have appeared the annual volumes of *Session Cases*. Details of other law literature can be found in David M. Walker (1981). Scottish Record Office indexes include a card index of unextracted processes 1675–1912 and copies of the Signet Library's *Index to Session Papers 1713–1820*.

The High Court of Justiciary holds a similar position in respect of criminal law to that held by the Court of Session in civil law. Indeed, the judges are the same in both instances. The institution grew out of the older Court of Justiciars, and in its present form dates from 1672. It has exclusive jurisdiction in cases of treason, murder, rape and incest, and also acts as appeal court from lower courts, expecially sheriff courts. One important feature is that, unlike the Court of Session, it sits in a number of towns apart from Edinburgh, for which purpose the country is divided into four circuits, each with its circuit towns. The court proceedings are recorded in *Books of Adjournal*.

One distinction which will often crop up is that between *solemn* and *summary* procedure. In the first, the case is heard before a jury; in the latter, for minor offences, the judge decides both verdict and penalty. In solemn procedure the charge is set out in a document called an *indictment*; in summary procedure in a *complaint*. Indictments are drawn up by procurators fiscal – officials of the crown, who prosecute on its behalf on the basis of *precognitions* (statements) from witnesses. The latter can be consulted among the archives of the Lord Advocate's department (AD) and themselves can be valuable material for the local historian.

Existing justiciary records begin in 1488, the circuit court system being preceded by justice-ayres. Selections have been published in Robert Pitcairn, *Criminal Trials in Scotland*, Bannatyne Club, 1833 (3 volumes), a fascinating source book covering the years 1488–1625. Proceedings between 1661 and 1678 have been published by the Scottish History Society, volume 1, 1903–4; volume 2, 1904–5; and more recently the Stair Society have published *Selected Justiciary Cases 1624–50* (1972). Nineteenth-century trials are covered in a series of volumes compiled by private reporters – listed in David M. Walker (1981). From 1874 justiciary cases have also been included in the annual *Session Cases*. One remarkable modern collection is that of William Roughead, who attended every important criminal trial at the High Court during his adult life. His papers are now held by the Signet Library, and some of them have been published as volumes in the *Notable Scottish Trials* series of William Hodge.

In this section on legal records to be found in the Scottish Record Office, we should also briefly mention the rich collection of registers, which will be discussed more fully in subsequent chapters in the context of the three major spheres of relevance: the individual, property and business. Registers have a varied provenance, but serve common functions which have been categorized as follows: *execution* (i.e. to give the grantee power of enforcement, the entry in the register being treated as if it were the verdict of a court); *preservation* (as in the case of agreements between parties, such as a marriage contract); and *publication* (in property transactions for example, so that prospective buyers will have the opportunity to establish that the seller has a valid claim to the title and has not alienated or burdened the property in any way). Some of these registers are still current, and the researcher must realize that they are in daily use by the legal profession, for whose benefit the legal search room is primarily provided. Normally search fees are charged, but these are waived in the case of bona-fide students.

Church records

The Normans, as well as importing the political system of feudalism into Scotland, also encouraged the introduction of continental religious institutions. Predominant were the monastic orders such as the Cistercians, who built up a reputation as agricultural pioneers, draining the bog lands of low-lying ground to create fertile plains. These monks differed from their Celtic predecessors in their employment of lay brothers for farming; the latter, being specialists, made unprecedented advances in scientific application. The monasteries received grants of land in the same way as barons, though often in the form of free and perpetual gifts – that is without the obligations of service imposed upon the former – which, given the chronic lawlessness of the time and the attendant calls upon the king's forces, was quite a considerable boon. The monasteries' value to the crown lay in other areas – in their role, in the words of T. B. Franklin (1952) as 'pioneer centres of law and order in a wild and turbulent country'. As far as local institutions were concerned, they were vested with the same authority as a baron, maintaining burghs of barony and even regalities (see pp. 53–5).

Monastic institutions were originally quite distinct from the Church's diocesan and parochial organization. There were 13 dioceses in Scotland, with two of them, Glasgow and St Andrews, divided into two archdeaconries. Subsequently monasteries began to acquire the benefices of parish churches (rich pickings were available from the 'teinds' – one-tenth of produce – charged to the parishioners for the upkeep of church and priest). Bishops, like abbots, could be major landowners.

The study of the pre-Reformation church is not one to be lightly undertaken by the amateur, at least not without some knowledge of Latin. Copies of some records are held by the Scottish Record Office (including papal bulls and sixteenth-century court archives), but the main repository in Scotland is the Roman Catholic Church's own archives, Columba House, 16 Drummond Place, Edinburgh EH3 6PL. A second major source is the Vatican Archives; at one time these would have been quite inaccessible to the amateur, but a prolonged labour on the part of the Department of History at Glasgow University has led to the identification and microfilming of pre-1560 material relating to Scotland. Glasgow's collection is described in I. B. Cowan, 'The Vatican Archives: a Report on Pre-

Reformation Material', *Scottish Historical Review*, vol. 48, 1969, pp. 227–42. Some source material has been published: papal letters 1201–1547 appear (in Latin) in A. Theiner, *Vetera Monumenta Hibernorum et Scotorum*, published in Rome, 1864, and calendars of papal letters have been produced by the Scottish History Society. Provincial legislation affecting Scotland is reproduced in *Statutes of the Scottish Church 1225–1559*, Scottish History Society, 1907. Details of monastic settlements are given in I.B. Cowan and D. E. Easson, *Religious Houses Scotland*, 2nd ed, Longman, 1976. Surviving monastic and diocesan records include charter books, registers and rentals, the latter often being the earliest source of information on the names and identities of local communities as well as providing an insight into the farming methods used. These records have been published almost without exception. Information about early parishes is contained in I. B. Cowan, *The Parishes of Medieval Scotland*, Scottish Record Society, 1967 (parishes were established throughout the country by the sixteenth century).

The Reformation swept away most of the institutions of the Catholic Church, and in their place the new Church of Scotland established a hierarchical structure of General Assembly, synod, presbytery and kirk session, all of which were both courts and administrative bodies. A complete break did not occur in that the ecclesiastical courts, known as commissary courts, as successors to the diocesan consistorial courts maintained a jurisdiction in marital and familial disputes, the execution of wills, slander and the taking of oaths, all of which were seen at the time as religious rather than civil concerns. Few of the records of the pre-Reformation courts survive; one published example is the *Liber Officialis Sancti Andree*, Abbotsford Club, 1844. The main value of commissary court records to the local historian – the social and family historian in particular – derives from the court's functions relating to the confirmation of testaments (wills) and the disposal of moveable estate (i.e. property other than land in general terms) in the case of both testate and intestate (i.e. where a will had not been made) succession. This subject is dealt with in more detail on pages 97–8.

The second major responsibility of the pre-Reformation courts – the consistorial jurisdiction (marriage contracts, divorce, separation and bastardy) – became the exclusive preserve of the Edinburgh Commissary Court, to whose records you must turn for information on any part of Scotland. They have been indexed under the title *The Commissariot of Edinburgh: Consistorial Processes and Decreets 1658–1800*, Scottish Record Society, 1909. In 1823 most of the commissary jurisdiction was transferred to the sheriff courts – a reflection of the erosion of church authority in the nineteenth century. Consistorial jurisdiction became the province of the Court of Session, though both terms – commissary and consistorial – are still used to describe these aspects of the respective courts' business.

The commissary courts themselves were finally abolished in 1876. Their records are deposited in the Scottish Record Office.

The new ecclesiastical structure set up at the Reformation encroached in other ways on what we would now regard as the civil domain. In this respect the parish kirk session was particularly important for, in the words of G. S. Pryde (1962) 'by virtue of all its new functions, the parish tended to take the place that had belonged to the medieval barony, as the handiest unit of rural administration'. These new functions included responsibility for poor relief – for which it could stent (tax) the parishioners if need be – the management of schools, and maintenance of registers of births, marriages and deaths. For the rest, it was particularly energetic in the punishment of adultery, sabbath breaking and alleged witchcraft. The kirk session acted under the general guidance of the commissioners of supply (see pages 60–1) and (in burghs) in co-operation with town councils. Expenditure required the involvement of yet another body, the heritors of the parish, whose number was made up by the major landowners. They paid for the upkeep of schools, manses and graveyards. Their records are held by the Scottish Record Office (HR) but do not on the whole predate the eighteenth century.

The parochial administrative tradition initiated by the kirk sessions was inherited by the civil authorities, who established parochial boards in 1845 to administer poor relief. Other powers too were lost in the nineteenth century, responsibility for schools, for example, being transferred to elected school boards in 1873. In this period of rapid change, the Church's own ecclesiastical administration was under strain, owing to the growth of urban populations, and there was a more widespread establishment of *quoad sacra* (meaning literally 'for sacred purposes only') parishes which did not perform the traditional civil duties of the older parishes.

The official repository for records of the Church of Scotland and of the various secessions now reunited with the main body is the Scottish Record Office. Published material includes the *Acts and Proceedings of the General Assembly 1560–1618*, Bannatyne Club: Maitland Club, 1839, and minute books of synod, presbytery and kirk session. The last-named are sometimes available on microfilm. Other religious denominations (Quakers, Methodists and Episcopalians) have followed the Church of Scotland in depositing their archives with the Scottish Record Office.

For the study of church buildings, there is the monumental work of D. MacGibbon and T. Ross, *The Ecclesiastical Architecture of Scotland*, David Douglas, 1896–7 (three volumes). In the present book, the section in Chapter Five on the study of buildings will also be generally applicable to churches. For early buildings, information can be gleaned from papal registers. Heritors' records will be relevant for church maintenance and building programmes.

The task of discovering information about ministers is one of the easiest a local researcher can be faced with, thanks to the existence of the *Fasti Ecclesiae Scoticanae*, which lists all ministers since the Reformation together with biographical data. The *Fasti* were originally published in the nineteenth century in seven volumes, and update supplements have been produced at intervals since. For the pre-Reformation period you can consult D. E. R. Watt, *Fasti Ecclesiae Scoticanae Medii Aevi ad Annum 1638*, Scottish Record Society, 1969 (second draft) and Charles H. Haws, *Scottish Parish Clergy at the Reformation 1540–1574*, Scottish Record Society, 1972. A series of volumes of Scottish supplications to Rome (applications for benefices – an unholy scramble in many cases) have been published by the Scottish History Society and latterly by Glasgow University Press. They cover the years 1418–1447 and contain a wealth of social information. Details are given in the Further Reading and Information section of this chapter. Presentations to benefices are recorded from 1488 in the Register of the Privy Seal (see page 124).

Church of Scotland records are of wider interest than the narrowly ecclesiastical. We have seen that its institutions were significant organs of social administration and that the kirk session was for two hundred years the only local parish body. During that period the General Assembly investigated and made recommendations on the social issues of the time, the reports showing similarities of character to royal commission reports. The importance of the church in the local community was reflected by the choice of the ministers to compile the statistical accounts; indeed, there is an earlier survey of 1627 for a limited number of parishes, conducted by the church itself (*Report on the State of Certain Parishes in Scotland . . . 1627*, Maitland Club, 1835).

Private records

Private archives are the most difficult about which to generalize, given their varied purpose and provenance. Three major categories can be roughly identified: family and estate papers, records of charitable institutions, and business archives. The first named is the largest group, and given the huge size, power and importance of landed estates in the rural landscape over many centuries, they can be tantamount to records of local administration. The contents can be multifarious – part of their fascination lies in the unexpected riches to be found, which may include marriage contracts, inventories of furnishings and clothes, estate plans, factors' accounts, 'tacks' (leases), rentals, 'teinds' (appropriated by the patrons of churches and by 'commendators' – laymen who inherited monastic estates), stipends, presentations to church benefices, household and personal accounts, letters, muniments (charters, etc.), contracts for building work, indentures (including apprenticeship agreements) and quite often the odd stray minute book or other item from a public archive. There are also many rolls of one kind or another – of fencible men, militia officers, justices of the peace, those receiving poor relief and estate workers – all of great value to the family historian.

If you have been disappointed by not finding a local record office in your neighbourhood, some compensation may be forthcoming in the shape of family or estate archives still preserved in their original setting. Such records have often not been consulted in great detail, and your study could break entirely new ground. You can check through the National Register of Archives or through local enquiry if there are papers held by local families, and you will need to make the approach yourself to obtain permission to use them. In most cases, they will probably not date much before the eighteenth century, so the handwriting should be manageable. You should however preface your study with background reading on eighteenth- and nineteenth-century farming practice.

The Scottish Record Office has huge collections of private archives (over 350), mainly engrossed in the category GD (Gifts and Deposits). The early inventories have been published in two volumes, *List of Gifts and Deposits in the Scottish Record Office*, HMSO, 1971, 1976, which it would be worthwhile to consult to gain some idea of the variety of material that can be included. This very diversity is the major problem associated with the use of private archives: there are few finding-aids to their contents, the absence being particularly inconvenient for those interested in a theme rather than a locality. The latter can be covered by an exhaustive check of the archives relating to one's neighbourhood, the identity of landowners through the centuries being established by means of the techniques outlined on pages 123–5. Progress, however, is being made all the time in indexing and assessing records; the Scottish Record Office, for example, continues to maintain its programme of source list compilation. The establishment of local record offices too will hopefully encourage a more substantial use and a consequent familiarity with the contents of private archives. The National Register of Archives includes some subject listings.

Local government records pre-1700

The earliest system of local government for which written records have survived is feudalism, introduced by the Normans to Scotland in the twelfth century. In a period when the nation states of Europe were still in the process of formation, it represented a solution to the problem of organizing a centralized state without the infrastructure – police, civil service or standing army – which permits the direct exercise of power by the authorities. Instead, feudalism was based upon a hierarchy, at the apex of which was the crown, the fountain of all justice and ultimate custodian of all land and resources. The monarch however devolved both judicial and territorial rights to the barons, his 'vassals', in return for certain services (originally 'knight's fee'). A charter is a document recording grants of land made under these conditions. The knight's fee was an undertaking to provide one or more knights to fight in the king's army when required, whilst the baron sometimes obtained in addition to his estates the right to hold a court, with civil and criminal jurisdiction over *his* vassals. The feudal system of land tenure has persisted in many respects to this day, the major modification being a commutation of knight's fee for a monetary payment known as 'feu-duty' (the vassal in this circumstance is called a 'feuar'). The two forms of tenure were called 'wardholding' and 'feuferme' respectively.

The hierarchical nature of the system is demonstrated by the fact that the baron in his turn could devolve parts of his estates (a barony was often co-extensive with a parish) and *his* vassals in turn could do likewise, a process known as 'subinfeudation'. Each individual could thus be at the same time the vassal of one and the superior of another, feudalism representing, according to David M. Walker (1981), a decentralized method of government, a system of land tenure, a military organization and a social and economic structure.

If the barony's charter included a clause of grant *in liberam baroniam*, the baron had the right to judicial as well as administrative powers, his court having civil competence in property disputes and debt and criminal competence for theft. Barony courts survived until 1747, though latterly they were but shadows of their former selves. But for centuries they constituted part of a legal system in which, in the words of P. Rayner et al. (1983), 'a large number of the king's subjects were not subject to the criminal jurisdiction of his courts, either at a central or a local level'. This observation applies with even more force to the regality courts, under the control of lords of regality, to which appeals from barony courts could be sent. A lord of regality was similar to a lord of barony but was vested with a jurisdiction almost as wide as that to be found in the king's court. A regality in fact could be called a state within a state.

The tally of surviving barony court records is paltry before the sixteenth century; and records that date from later periods consist mainly of trifling matters such as breaches of the peace, fines for non-attendance at court, and compulsory labour on the 'mains' (i.e. landowner's) farm. An early published record is that of Carnwath (from 1523) the volume being prefaced with an essay on the history of barony courts; extracts from Forbes and Urie court books have also been reproduced. Scottish Record Office holdings are listed in P. Rayner et al. (1983) and inventory RH11 is also devoted to the subject.

Within the feudal system a special position was accorded to the burghs, which had their own system of land tenure known as 'burgage'. The barony was basically geared towards a subsistence economy: the role of the burghs was to sponsor economic activity as trading and craft manufacturing centres. Such pursuits meant income for the crown through taxation (port customs and 'petty' customs from produce sold in the markets). Collection of petty customs was the responsibility of 'king's' bailies' (*ballivi regis*) who also collected 'maills' (annual rent on burgesses' properties). Later, bailies became burgh officials, and income from petty customs was retained by the burghs in exchange for feu-duties or *reddendo* paid to the crown. The burghs got the better of the bargain – the feu-duties were fixed in perpetuity. Collection of petty customs itself was administratively difficult, and was often farmed out at public 'roupings' (auctions). Published lists of petty customs are often found in library local history collections and can be used for a study of the economic situation of the day.

Burghs were also frequently granted monopolies over trade within their hinterland, areas known as their 'liberties'. Restrictive practices benefited both the merchants, who excluded competitors and milked the surrounding populace, and the king, who was able to keep close control through his Exchequer.

Burghs were often established by royal charter, holding lands, like barons, direct from the crown, in which case they were known as 'royal' burghs. They were given exclusive control of foreign trade and acquired a further privilege, that of electing from among their elite – the merchants or burgesses – magistrates (a provost, bailies, treasurer and dean of guild) to officiate at the burgh court and later to be the office bearers of a town council.

In addition to the royal burghs, two other types of burgh evolved – the 'burgh of barony' and the 'burgh of regality' – differing from royal burghs in that they were not erected by the king but by barons and lords of regality respectively under royal grant. They had similar commercial privileges to the royal burghs, but often no elected council and little access to foreign trade. Both burghs of barony and burghs of regality could be and frequently were raised to royal rank, though in the earliest recorded periods there was no clear distinction between the different categories of burgh.

A large number of burghs of barony were erected in the sixteenth and seventeenth centuries. They were intended, according to G. S. Pryde (1962) 'to meet the needs of the country dwellers and the village folk for some shopping facilities and for the services of the humbler kind of craftsmen at no unreasonable distance from their homes . . . without any obligation on him [the landowner] or on the local community to establish and maintain a burgh'. In other words, the interests of trade were paramount, not requirements of burghal administration or local democracy. For the local historian the important point to bear in mind is that the setting up of a burgh of barony was not necessarily accompanied by an administrative framework, and there will not always be any local records to throw light on its development.

One point to note in the study of burghs is that most were extremely small and in no way resembled what we understand by a town today. Even important royal burghs often had only a few hundred inhabitants at the end of the eighteenth century. At the same time, they are important to an understanding of the evolution of Scottish local government, which maintained, up to as late as 1974, a dual system, with major differences between the administration of burghs and of landward areas. Burghs are also significant in the growth of a modern economy, though this feature must not be over-stressed.

Surviving burgh records are much richer than those of barony courts. Charters were jealously preserved as proof of economic and territorial rights, and many have been published, together with other documents relating to burghal privileges. They are also recorded in the Register of the Great Seal (see page 124). This said, charters are often couched in formalistic language which tells us little about specific local circumstances, though it is interesting to try to plot the local topography from the description of marches. A list of cartularies is given in W. Angus (1936). Archaeological data and town council minutes can be utilized for a more detailed re-construction of an early burgh's layout – suggestions on how such a project could proceed are outlined in Chapter Six.

The burgh's court fulfilled roughly the same functions as the barony court in landward areas, enforcing regulations and settling disputes, though it was also responsible for registering property and business transactions. A possible project would be to compare the operations of burgh and barony courts. Surviving records of the former are discussed in D. Robertson and M. Wood (1936).

The competence of the courts was restricted by the rise of the king's own system of courts, by which time, however, they had assumed administrative powers that became vested in town councils familiar to us from later periods. It is the minute books of the latter, with their wealth of social and economic information, that afford us the most detailed insight into local life before the eighteenth century. The oldest surviving records are for Aberdeen (from 1398). Edinburgh's date from 1403, Peebles's from 1456 and Lanark's from 1488. Publication, in full or in extracts, was associated particularly with the Scottish Burgh Records Society, but also, as in the case of Edinburgh, with the town councils themselves. Also to be consulted for bibliographical information is A. J. Mill (1923), though his list of council records is not exhaustive.

Other administrative records include minute books of merchant guilds and craft incorporations (roughly equivalent to trade unions), records of admission of burgesses, accounts of burgh treasurers, customs records, and 'common good' accounts, of which there are some sixteenth- and seventeenth-century survivals in the Exchequer archives. Common good consisted of profits from burghal lands; the money was used for policing, tollbooths, trons (the official town weights) and fortifications. Together with the petty customs mentioned above and other indirect taxes, such as that on the sale of beer, the profit from common good obviated in most cases the need for direct local taxation in burghs. The only other substantial burden on the burgesses (apart from army service) was that of 'watching and warding'.

All these records could be used to explore the origins of burgh pageantry and heraldry: today their functions are ceremonial, but they arose from economic and political exigencies. A fault of which the local historian is sometimes guilty is that of placing undue emphasis on the burgh's heritage (reflecting his pride in his town) without realizing that today's traditions are in large measure the ossified survivals of the power struggles of the past.

A secondary burgh court was the dean of guild court which had jurisdiction in matters of building control and nuisance (aspects of environmental health which are still prominent in local government today). Another published source is the records of the Convention of the Royal Burghs 1552–1779. Burghs were originally granted representation in the Scottish Parliament in the fourteenth century, burgesses becoming one of the three estates. The privilege was restricted to royal burghs, and the Convention of the Royal Burghs evolved from their need to co-ordinate parliamentary strategy.

A point that needs to be repeated is that there is little value in the amateur local historian aspiring to be a medievalist: in ninety-nine cases out of a hundred he is not going to be in a position to make a significant contribution to the debates and problems involved. The surviving records are sketchy and the connections between them disjointed. The medievalist must work in a national context and his study may hinge on the crucial interpretation of a text or obscure office, say in relation to burgh organization. If the amateur burgh historian enters the argument, he is liable either to repeat the scrap of information without having any idea of its meaning – a pointless exercise – or, even worse, will attempt an explanation which is totally misleading. The introduction to Margaret Stuart's *Guide* (1930) gives a detailed example of the quagmires awaiting the amateur who attempts such a task.

The records to be used by the local historian must satisfy three criteria: they must have bulk, they must have continuity, and the function of the institutions concerned must be quite clear. Few if any medieval records fulfil these requirements. Continuity is particularly important, for it ensures that the content of the records, which is what is of local value, outweighs any consideration of their provenance and significance.

The unsuitability of early records is exacerbated when the local historian is unsure of his purpose, the common mistake being to fall for what we may term 'the chronological fallacy'. This is the mistake of viewing the historian's task as that of drawing a thread through time from the years when records begin up to the present day. So, for example, in the study of a village, such a researcher finds mention of a benefice granted in 1265, a charter from 1390, a writ from 1352, and these scraps he dutifully records in his history. Now the idea that this jumble of assorted facts constitutes an early history of the village is totally false. The unfounded assumption is that to have discovered a fact – any fact – from each century solves the problem of continuity. But why each century? Why not each year or each week? And even if one could find a piece of information for each week, the essential element – a causal connection between them – would still be missing. The chronological fallacy is doubly dangerous in that it invites other errors: the vacuum left by the lack of continuity encourages the local historian to fill it with bland nonsense, uninformed prejudices or comments from his own contemporary experience.

If one had to choose a time when Scottish records first become sufficiently substantial to be of use to the local historian, it would be the beginning of the sixteenth century, when Scotland emerged from a long dark age. From that time burgh records have a continuous history, though in certain landward areas we must resign ourselves to the fact that even up to the middle of the seventeenth century, there is not much to show, if we are seeking details of local administration which allow us to identify specific individuals and developments. For the study of these areas and all areas in medieval times, other methods drawn from archaeology and geography must be used – they are discussed further in Chapters Five and Six.

As well as barony and burgh records, there is a third group of local records that pre-date the Union, those of the sheriff courts. The sheriffs, who were officials appointed from among the Scoto-Norman barons, acted as the king's local judicial, financial and administrative representatives. Sheriffdoms were first erected in the twelfth and thirteenth centuries, the sheriff court being held at the baron's castle, but as the burghs grew up under its protecting walls, the head of the sheriffdom came to be the burgh itself, even though the sheriff at that time had no jurisdiction within its boundaries. By the sixteenth century, the tollbooth was the site of the court – which marks an interesting development for a building that originated as a booth at the burgh's fair where dues or tolls were collected. Tollbooths also came to serve as the sheriffdoms' prisons, which can be studied via the burgh incarceration books, where these have survived. In the counties 'rogue money' was charged on freeholders to help defray costs. Empty tollbooth prisons are still registered in nineteenth-century census enumeration books, by which time a state system had been introduced. The latter can be investigated in the

Scottish Record Office HH files which include prison registers from 1657 and records of the county prison boards (up to 1877) and the Prison Commission 1839–1929. Two early nineteenth-century eyewitness accounts are J. Neild (1812) and J. J. Gurney (1819). In rural areas prisons were the responsibility of the commissioners of supply (see pp. 60–61).

The association of the sheriffdom with the head burgh of an area marks a stage in the evolution of shires or counties as we understand them: for the sheriff was not only responsible for civil and criminal justice, but also fulfilled a large number of administrative functions, including executing royal writs, repairing castles, guarding prisoners and controlling beggars. Collective responsibility was involved too, in that all the barons were expected to attend the court.

The oldest sheriff court records now extant date only from the sixteenth century, and it is only in a few cases – Aberdeen, Linlithgow, Haddington, Perth and Fife – that they extend even that far back. The Aberdeen record (from 1503) has been published by the New Spalding Club. Renfrew's and Fife's are among other published sources, the latter being prefaced by an important essay on early sheriff courts (for details, see the Further Reading and Information section). Regarding the use of sheriff records, it must be remembered that the sheriffdom's jurisdiction was not co-extensive with the county. This only became the case in 1747 when the private and exclusive jurisdictions of regalities were abolished. Sheriff court records (SC) are deposited mainly with the Scottish Record Office, though some devolution to local record offices has taken place.

The rise of county government 1700–1850

In many respects the Union with England in 1707 was a watershed in the history of Scottish government. Scotland, because of her relatively backward economy, entered the Union with a considerable residue of feudal institutions, especially in the continuing practice of delegating administrative and judicial powers to the nobility. By the eighteenth century there were around 200 baronies and regalities (all heritable) and the problem was compounded by the fact that many of the sheriffdoms too had become hereditary. It is true that some regalities had 'escheated' to the king (i.e. the lands had been forfeited) and were administered directly by the king through his bailie as 'stewartries' or 'bailiaries'; and also that baronies and regalities themselves had lost most of their judicial powers through abeyance, though some executive duties remained (conserving common lands and woods and maintaining dykes and ditches). However, such a system hardly provided the infrastructure necessary for the development of a modern state, and it became even more unsatisfactory from the authorities' point of view after the Jacobite rebellions of 1715 and 1745, when the loyalties of many of the Scots nobility were called into question. Thus in 1747 baronies and regalities to all intents and purposes were abolished. They were replaced on the one hand by a collective authority of landowners acting as justices of the peace and commissioners of supply, and on the other by an extension of the power of government officials. The hereditary sheriffdoms were also discontinued, though the office of sheriff itself was not: it became a nominal post for prestige only, power being entrusted to the sheriff depute (a lawyer) and his assistants, known as sheriff substitutes. Local administration was handled by the sheriff clerk.

The new sheriff deputes had wide-ranging responsibilities in addition to those inherited from the older sheriffs. They included accounting for crown dues, calling jurors, managing parliamentary elections and striking the fiars (grain prices). The powers of the sheriff court had already been strengthened in the seventeenth century, when for the first time inhabitants of royal burghs had become liable to prosecution there if accused of other than trivial offences. The burgh courts (renamed burgh police courts under the Burgh Police Acts of 1892 and 1903) survived until 1975 when they were abolished, together with the justice of the peace courts (their rough equivalents in landward areas), which likewise had come to have jurisdiction only in matters of breach of the peace and other petty charges. Since 1975 the duties of both courts have been performed by a new district court.

With its new responsibilities and an extension of jurisdiction into regalities, the sheriff court became, along with the Court of Session and Justiciary Court, the framework within which all significant legal actions were considered; and its powers were widened even further in 1822 when the jurisdictions of the church commissary courts were transferred to it. Administrative duties too were increased to include inspection of prisons and asylums, fatal accident enquiries and confirmation of local authority bye-laws. The full extent of these powers was detailed in the evidence to the Royal Commission on the Court of Session and the Office of Sheriff Principal (1927).

The modern sheriff court is competent in cases of debt and damages, landlord and tenant disputes, separation, breach of contract and succession. Divorce and legitimacy are excluded, being the preserve of the Court of Session. Company law remit is restricted to smaller capital flotation. In criminal cases, the court tries crimes for which a conviction of two years' imprisonment or less can be enforced. There are at present six sheriffdoms, subdivided into 50 districts (roughly the old Scottish counties, whose identity they helped to create before the progressive amalgamation of sheriff-doms). The records of the court fall into three categories, *civil*, *commissary* and *criminal*. The civil category includes minute books and act books, registers of ordinary and summary actions, processes and registers of decrees. A whole group of records relate to creditor/debtor law and are discussed in Chapter Six. Criminal records include indictments, summary complaints and diet books. 'Diet' refers to the process of prosecution, which takes place in two stages. The first diet is held at the sheriff court and the accused states whether he wishes to plead guilty; if there is to be a trial, it is set for the second diet, which can take place either in the sheriff court or High Court of Justiciary, depending on the gravity of the offence.

The post-1747 *sheriffdoms* were one of four institutions on which county government was based, the others being *lieutenancies* and the collective authorities of *justices of the peace* and *commissioners of supply*. The justice of the peace was an English institution, introduced into Scotland in 1609 by James VI. In the seventeenth century this import made little impact, and in 1708 an attempt was made to strengthen the office by granting it larger-scale administrative powers: to settle disputes over work and wages, to oversee weights and measures, working hours and conditions of service, to suppress riots, to control poaching, to take oaths and to supervise prisons and almshouses. To these were added others in 1718, for example the responsibility, in conjunction with the commissioners of supply, for organizing the maintenance of country roads, for controlling vagabonds and for ensuring the smooth operations of poor law regulations; though this sharing of power, both with the commissioners and with sheriffs, is one reason why the institution was never really successfully grafted on to the Scottish system. Alongside there was also established the subordinate office of constable, to which a man was appointed in each village. Its status can be summed up in the following description of the duties by Ann E. Whetstone (1981): 'delivering a citation to a man in the next village and asking around after stray dogs, unburied dead horses and idlers'. The justices of the peace, who comprised the main landowners (gentry now as well as the older nobility), held district courts (or were supposed to) from which there was appeal to the quarter or general sessions of the county, where all the justices met together. Fear of civil unrest led to quite large extensions in their numbers – to nearly 5,600 by 1830, by which time their membership was being broadened by the appointment of merchants and industrial entrepreneurs. They had been given further responsibilities – for small debt claims and for licensing, in which area new and more stringent regulations were introduced in the Forbes Mackenzie Act of 1853, and they remained with these functions up to 1974, but with little else. The court records (JP) are held by the Scottish Record Office and some regional and district archive offices. They cover the years 1613–1975. The licensing records can be valuable in tracing the history of public houses.

The post of commissioner of supply was another seventeenth-century introduction which came into its own in the eighteenth. The commissioners consisted of a committee of wealthy landowners of the county appointed originally to allocate the 'cess' or land tax amongst their peers; and because they constituted a ready-made forum for local opinion, it became convenient to entrust them with other duties, such as the enforcement of the Education Act of 1696 and responsibilities for roads and bridges. They represented the gentry rather than nobility, and as such they helped to develop a county consciousness, expressing the local view on such issues as the corn laws, internal defence and Scottish bills passing through Parliament.

In 1854 the Valuation of Lands Act instituted the annual valuation of property (the current rates system), thus undermining the central function of the commissioners, though the latter had been empowered to adopt the Police Act of 1839 (see page 64), bringing them within the new local government structure of the post-1832 era. However, the establishment of a limited local democracy under the new system, in which ownership of large areas of land ceased to be a prerequisite of participation, made the office progressively anomalous, and reforms were set in train that culminated in the establishment of elected bodies, the county councils, in 1889. The latter inherited from the commissioners many of the traditions of county government, and indeed many of their buildings as well. The inherent conservatism of institutions is demonstrated by the fact that the office was not abolished in 1889, the commissioners working in harness with county councillors on joint police committees up to 1929. You might like to make this cautiousness in change a subject of study.

The lieutenant was yet a third import from England, the introduction originating from English doubts as to the loyalty of the Scots to the new Hanoverian monarchy. Scots nobles were chosen but the posts were not permanent. The lieutenant's task was to organize civil defence and to report on disorders; but until the time of the Napoleonic Wars the mistrust of the Scots was such that the authorities were afraid to grant extensive powers. It was the threat of invasion in the 1790s that finally forced a change, and permanent lieutenancies were established, with powers to raise and direct militia and volunteers. The militia system was that whereby the civil population was obliged to register and be called upon for civil defence duties. Hitherto in Scotland 'fencible units' had been used for this purpose; these were raised by noblemen on special commission from the king and were composed of volunteers who enlisted only for the duration of a war and were limited to home service. The emergency of the Napoleonic Wars led to 33 separate fencible infantry units being raised between 1793 and 1802; and the same crisis led to the establishment of militia forces under the Scottish Militia Act 1797, which was the cause of serious rioting as the populace resisted enrolment. That the Militia Act was needed reflected the failure of volunteer forces, which the lieutenants were also encouraged to raise. These were mostly disbanded after 1808 and the term 'volunteers' became almost synonymous with 'yeomanry' (volunteer cavalry). Yeomanry came from a higher social stratum (those who could maintain horses) and were used to repress the civil disorder which was prevalent in the years 1815–30. The rise of the police forces under the various Police Acts of the following years finally led to the eclipse of yeomanry and of the lieutenants who organized them.

The commissioners of supply and lieutenancy records form part of county council archives. The former are the more extensive, the general minute books being supplemented by minute books of a police committee in those areas where they adopted police acts, and by records of roads trustees (often based on parishes), which are discussed further in Chapter Six.

Perhaps the most widespread and valuable primary sources from the eighteenth century onwards are the minute books of institutions and their various committees. Two observations can be made on their use: first, background information on the participants will add an extra dimension to your understanding (their motivation, for example, will become apparent); secondly, rather than wading through from cover to cover, it is best to try to identify recurring patterns and preoccupations which you can exemplify by copying relevant extracts under chosen headings. The next stage of your work is then to analyse what they tell you about the fundamental orientation of the institution. Or perhaps the recurring pattern is a sign of frustration, the members returning repeatedly to an issue about which dissatisfaction persists.

The eighteenth century is the first period for which the study of the administration of landward areas can be confidently undertaken. You might want to look at the overall administrative framework of a parish in any one year, comparing kirk session minutes, heritors' records, justice of the peace minutes and commissioner of supply records. Or you might prefer to pursue a theme through the century: policing would be an interesting topic which could be studied through a variety of archives – sheriff court, commissioner of supply, justice of the peace, lieutenancy and volunteer regiments. You could look at the civil disturbance of the early nineteenth century and investigate the extent to which its policing reflected the political and economic interests of the ruling group. A comparison could be made with the period subsequent to the introduction of the police forces. Were new principles of impartiality established at the outset, and if so, who was responsible for laying them down? Another topic would be to consider improvements to the environment carried out by local government bodies. Roads would be the best example. Did those who superintended their maintenance fully appreciate the economic significance of what they were doing? Do we find the agriculture improvers of the area pushing for better facilities and local landowners willing to pay for them? In other words, did they have a concept of the potentiality of local government? Another project would be to monitor the changing composition of county institutions during this period in terms of class, profession and status within the community. Did, for example, the widening of the franchise in 1832 lead to different patterns of power?

Local government records 1832–present

The nineteenth century saw greater changes in our way of life in a short period of time than any previous era. The root cause was the industrial revolution, one consequence of which was the concentration of large numbers of people in urban environments, leading to an unprecedented need for services such as water supply, sanitation, lighting, planning and so on, which had not been an important feature of traditional local government. The urban areas in some cases corresponded with existing burghs, but in others sprang up rapidly out of the countryside. Even where there were burghs, the councils had long since become corrupt and dominated by self-perpetuating cliques who had the sole choice in determining their successors. So the problem was threefold: to reform the government of existing burghs, to introduce burgh-type government to new urban communities, and to extend the range of local government functions.

The widening of the franchise in the royal burghs and the eclipse of the ruling elites came in 1833, under the momentum generated by the victory of the parliamentary reformers in 1832. Under a statute of that year, town councils were to be elected by all householders with property valued at £10. The 1832 act had other repercussions too: traditionally parliamentary seats had had a limited electorate and most of the royal burghs had been grouped in fours and fives to elect an MP. Part of the extension of suffrage was achieved by the erection of new groups of 'parliamentary burghs' to return their own MPs, and under an 1833 Act such burghs were given powers comparable to those found in royal burghs.

Royal burghs, burghs of barony, parliamentary burghs and other 'populous places' (a population of as little as 700 sufficing after 1862) were also permitted by successive legislation to adopt a policing system (understood in its widest sense to include lighting, paving, cleansing, water supply and public order). These powers were granted between 1833 and 1862, though some burghs had adopted the system earlier through private acts of Parliament. Such burghs became 'police burghs', in which authority was entrusted to police commissioners and police magistrates, who might or might not be the same as bailies and councillors. In other words, some burghs carried two administrations simultaneously, responsible for different aspects of local government (this was a solution to the problem of burgh corruption). The dual system lasted until the end of the nineteenth century, when the Burgh Police (Scotland) Acts 1892 and 1903 and the Town Councils (Scotland) Act 1900 coordinated all functions in the hands of around 200 burghs, thus effectively ending a centuries' old distinction between royal burghs and burghs of barony. New distinctions were soon to arise, however, for the Local Government (Scotland) Act 1929 recognized no less than three types of burgh: counties of cities (Edinburgh, Glasgow, Aberdeen and Dundee) which were responsible for all the functions of a county council; large burghs (originally those with a population in excess of 20,000) who exercised most of the functions of a county council with the major exception of education; and small burghs, whose functions included only housing, sanitation, management of local roads, licensing, burials and consumer protection.

Up to the time of local government re-organization in 1974–5, given the different sizes of authority and their overlapping responsibilities, joint councils, committees and boards proliferated. In some areas, for example water supply, police or social services, the researcher is faced with a bewildering array of bodies. The tables reproduced on pages 146–53 will hopefully assist in clarifying the main outlines. For more detailed information, the student is advised to consult textbooks of local government administrative law written at different key points over the last 100 years (listed in the Further Reading and Information section of this chapter).

In the counties there were many parallel developments. Just as populous places could adopt the police acts and elect police commissioners, so in the rural areas the commissioners of supply could adopt the police acts under legislation of 1839 and 1857. At the same time some completely new institutions were created, of a more democratic character than hitherto. Parochial boards based on the parish unit were set up in 1845 and included the burghs that lay within their boundaries. They comprised elected members, kirk session delegates, heritors and burgh magistrates, and their main function was to operate the conditions of the Poor Law Act of 1845 by organizing poor relief. In 1867 the pioneering Public Health (Scotland) Act gave parochial boards further duties relating to public health and water supply (mostly transferred to the new county councils in 1889). The Act also permitted the creation of 'special districts' within counties for purposes of water supply and sewerage (lighting and scavenging were added later) to accommodate the requirements of villages which were not large enough to become police burghs but which needed many of the services which police burghs offered. Special districts became part of the county council structure in 1889 and were not abolished until 1974.

In 1894, under the continuing pressure towards democracy, the functions of the parochial boards were mostly transferred to a new body, the parish council, which was fully elected. This followed the pattern of elected school boards, which had been set up in 1872 in each burgh and parish with powers to levy a local rate for education and responsibility for the management of schools. In 1878 county road trustees had become the roads' authority, the older statute roads system and turnpike trusts being abolished. The logical conclusion of these various developments was the formation of elected bodies with general supervisory powers in rural areas – the county councils. These were initially established in 1889, taking over most of the functions of the commissioners of supply, justices of the peace and county road trustees, for which they were given powers to levy a comprehensive rate. In larger counties, 'district committees' (comprising local councillors and one parish councillor from each parish and burgh) acted as their agents in matters affecting roads and public health.

In 1929 the county councils took over those boards still remaining with a specialized remit and the parish councils and district committees were disbanded. Some powers could henceforth be delegated to a new body, the 'district council' (not to be confused with the post-1974 district councils – these latter are the successors to the county councils). The district councils of 1929–74 were independent local authorities with minor powers, but they also served as agents for the county council in some local matters.

The 1974 changes in local government were a radical departure, in that the centuries-old distinction between burgh and landward areas was abolished. A single system of government now applies to all areas, with a two-tier arrangement of regional councils (very large authorities: nine altogether in Scotland plus three Island authorities) with powers over education, roads, social services and structure planning; and district councils (53 in all, roughly covering the areas of former county councils) with responsibilities for housing, environmental health, leisure and recreation, and local planning. To represent local opinion, community councils (with no statutory powers) have been established.

County council archives engross those of all the boards and councils taken over at different times, including the commissioners of supply, parochial boards and school boards. All joint board records are also included with county council records rather than town council records. The county council's own archives will contain the minute books of various sub-committees, such as the education committee or animal diseases committee.

Suggested projects

The researcher will have no difficulty in making a study of any of the specific functions of local government over the last 150 years, be it police, water supply, fire services, housing or public health. In many areas, too, the student will have the choice of an engineering or a social viewpoint. You could also make a study of the concept of local government itself and how it came to prevail – newspaper correspondence will throw light on changing attitudes to administration. Town planning would be one theme that could be investigated in this context. What were town planners trying to achieve at different periods, and how effectively did they control or channel the impulses of developers?

In the study of present-day conurbations such as Glasgow, you will find that the records of previously independent burghs will be relevant, as the latter were gradually encroached upon and finally swallowed up by their larger neighbours. An interesting project would be to study the response of the town councils involved, and to monitor their attempts to preserve their identity. Such a study could be complemented by a geographical examination of structural alterations in the landscape that perhaps follow on from the loss of administrative independence – this theme is pursued further in Chapter Six.

You could make a study of local politics – from the late nineteenth century, as suffrage was widened, local councillors increasingly identified themselves with party viewpoints. To supplement the minute books of councils, you could use local newspapers, political leaflets and the sometimes quite vitriolic pamphlets that were circulated.

Sometimes the letter books of councils have survived and can be used alongside the minutes – they will give a view of specific cases which were discussed only in general terms at council meetings. It is interesting to contrast the outlook of the official and the councillor – their respective responses to new concepts such as council housing, or to strains upon existing services, as in the 1930s, when high levels of unemployment threatened poor relief provision, still at that time a local government function. What ideology motivated the officials, and did they lead or follow their political masters? Such a study could be extended to an examination of the social class and background of councillors and officials.

1 Stirling around 1690 – a typically panoramic view from Slezer's *Theatrum Scotiae*. The town, like many others, is dominated by its church and castle. The layout of many burghs can be investigated in Slezer's prints, which are also valuable for their portrayal of the surrounding countryside. Note here the enclosed orchard or garden, a sign of the influence of the improving movement.

2 A broadsheet anonymously produced in the wake of the Ravensheugh Toll Riot of 1760. The satirist lampoons the drunken English soldiers who had beaten a toll-keeper and his wife when returning to their barracks. A good example of how yesterday's ephemera become fascinating documents for today's local historian.

3 A print of Inverness from *Scotland Illustrated*, published by George Virtue in 1838. The drawing is by Thomas Allom and the engraving by R. Sands. The riverside location is common among burghs, as is the 'sub-urb' situated on the opposite bank and originally outwith the jurisdiction of the burgh. Contrast the romantic treatment of the group around the piper with the photographic reality in the next illustration.

THE

SURPRISING and HEROIC

ATCHIEVEMENT

A T

Ravenshaugh Toll.

To refcue from the Jaws of Oblivion or vague Tradition, and to hand down to Pofterity, unfullied by the noxious Blafts of Envy or Malice, an Atchievement more perilous and more tremenduous than the moft renowned of the peerlefs Knight of LA MANCHA, *is the difinterefted Motive of ufhering into the World the following impartial Narrative.*

Ecce fpectaculum Deo dignum————

ON the Evening of *Sunday,* the 5th Day of *October* 1760, fome Officers of Light Dragoons, who had been out on a foraging Party as far as *Haddington,* were returning to their Cantonment at *Mufleburgh.* The Toll-bar, within a Mile of the laft mentioned Place, had been feized upon, that very Day, by a Party of *French* *; who, with the Policy and Craft characteriftic of their Nation, difguifed themfelves in the Habits of Women, all except their Commandant, who affumed the Drefs and

A   Character

---

* Some People, more inquifitive than wife, doubt of this Fact; becaufe they have not heard how thefe *French* arrived on our ifland: To which we anfwer, that if it be fo, that the *French* did take Poffeffion of *Ravenfhaugh* Toll-houfe, it is of no confequence whether they came from *France* on the Back of a Fifh, in a Flat-bottomed Boat, or a Nut-fhell.

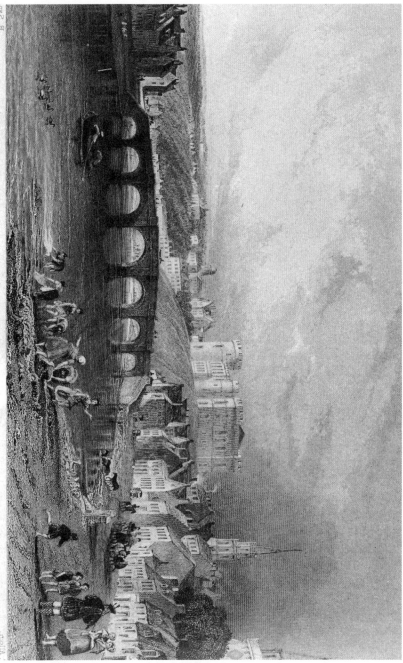

4 A street busker photographed by William Graham in 1898 in Prestonpans near Edinburgh. An archive of Graham's photographs is held by Glasgow District Libraries. Note the water pump and the tenements with outside stairs. The tenement was typical of the Scottish industrial landscape (attributable in part to the existence of feu duties on land). In 1871 over 70 per cent of Scotland's population lived in one or two roomed dwellings, mostly in tenements of three or four storeys.

5 The *Shire of Lenox or Dunbarton* from Moll's *Set of Thirty Six New and Correct Maps of Scotland Divided into Shires*, published in 1725 and based on surveys by Pont, Gordon and Adair. Early county maps can be used to identify small settlements that were either moved or disappeared during and after enclosure. Larger scale county maps from later in the eighteenth century often indicate enclosed estates and their policies.

The Shire of
LENOX or
DUNBARTON

By H. Moll Geographer.

Miles of Great Britain 60 to a D.

Loch Lomund
Famous for its
Floting Island its
Fish without Fins.
and being frequ
ently Tempestu
ous in a Calm

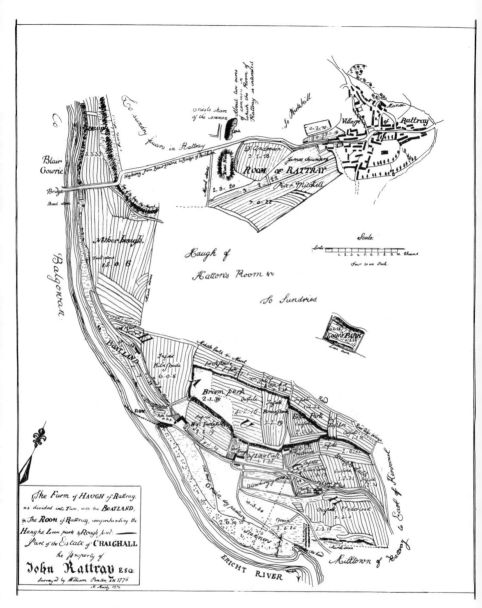

6 Part of a copy of an estate plan of Rattray in East Perthshire (RHP 41445 Ex GD 385) dated 1776. This eighteenth-century village was a centre for hand-loom weavers – note the bleaching greens, mill lade and the 'good, new-built mill' (for scutching or heckling the flax). Infield, outfield and commons are also shown. The legend 'sundry feuars in Rattray' indicates that in this area small plots of land had been feud to small proprietors – a practice used by landowners to acquire ready cash.

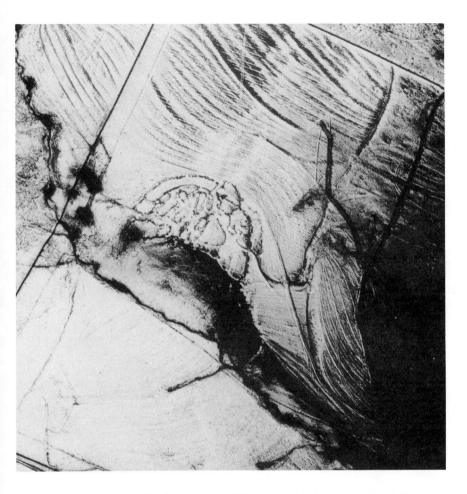

7 A vanished local landscape revealed from an aerial photograph taken after
snow. The township of Lour in Peebleshire is shown as an abandoned site on
an estate plan of 1794. The outerworks of the settlement are from the early
Iron Age, and the township of medieval and post-medieval date. Also
featured are rig cultivation patterns which sweep across current field
boundaries. Full analysis of the rig patterns is given in the Royal Commission
on the Ancient and Historical Monuments of Scotland's *Inventory for
Peebleshire*.

8 Part of John Wood's *Plan of Dunbar* 1830, showing a typical small royal burgh laid out along a single wide street, often leading originally up to a castle gate (as is probably the case here). Behind the tenements are strips of land known as 'tofts' – even in towns, a rural pattern of life was maintained. As burghs grew, alleyways or pends were cut from the main street and houses built at right-angles to it along the tofts. Note the naming of proprietors – a boon to family and social historians.

Chapter Four

THE INDIVIDUAL AND THE COMMUNITY

This chapter is concerned with the people of local history, seen from a variety of viewpoints – those of the genealogist, the oral historian and the social historian. The family researcher will be particularly identified by his interest in registers, but equally there are ways of exploiting the same sources to explore the workings of a local community. The social historian will want to investigate the environment in which our forebears lived – schooling, work, social welfare – but the genealogist can use such information as biographical background to the individuals in his family tree. The oral historian actively contributes towards an extension of historical source material, providing the social historian with an unofficial witness of an age to set against the written records of public bodies. The work of all the specialists can together contribute to an understanding of the bonds – of kinship, religion and social and economic institutions – which constitute a community. The chapter also considers some methodological problems, such as bias in the historian. For it is in the realm of social studies that we encounter our own strongly held beliefs, which can distort our historical judgement. The warning is apposite, as too many amateur pieces of research are marred by moral, religious and political stances that have no place in a social science such as history.

Family history

The fascination of local history is nowhere more strongly felt than in the search for one's own forebears. It is easy to understand and appreciate why this is so. The family is a direct link to the past, and through it we can enter sympathetically into the lives of others who inhabited worlds much different from our own, yet at the same time observe how today's circumstances are fashioned, both physically and mentally, by their actions. The first discovery of the would-be historian is that the past is a force acting on our every move and thought, our social and political selves. By the same token, we anchor ourselves firmly in our traditions, narrow family traditions as well as broader social ones. The consciousness of and fascination with the links between past and present which enthuse the family researcher also motivate the local historian in the other areas of research we shall be considering.

The first step in a genealogical project is to exploit the sources close at hand – the photographs, mementoes, documents and reminiscences of your living relatives. The researcher should constantly be aware of the fact that material for historical study is to be found not only in libraries, museums and record offices but also in the local community and landscape. The most challenging task is that of interviewing your relatives, to discover what they can tell you about themselves, their parents and grandparents. To this end you must decide initially on the questions to which you are wanting an answer: your interviewees will vary in their capacity to express themselves logically and to the point. If you cannot provide a structure for them, the encounter can degenerate into irrelevant gossip. The recommended procedure is to compile a checklist of facts which you want to establish about each individual; it will include date and place of birth, siblings, date of marriage, wife or husband and children. When you actually go to see each relative, you should take with you a sheaf of cards or A4 sheets marked at the top with the name of the person you are interviewing and down the side with the items from the checklist. A separate sheet should be used not only for each interviewee, but also for each individual about whom they give you information. This procedure effectively ensures conformity to two basic rules of historical research: notes must always be taken in such a way that they can be easily manipulated for purposes of comparison; and secondly, the source of any piece of information should always be apparent. This applies equally to written sources and oral witness.

Once you have completed your interviews, you should already have quite a few cards or sheets dealing with some of your recent ancestors. Your next job is to collate the information about each individual, checking as you do so for discrepancies between one account and another. Where these occur, they should be noted in readiness for the second phase of your project, consultation of the official registers. These are to be found in the General Register Office for Scotland, New Register House, Edinburgh EH1 3YT (telephone: 031 556 3952). This building is next door to the Scottish Record Office, but set back to one side. It is sometimes a source of confusion that the Scottish Record Office's address is HM General Register House (or Old Register House); the General Register Office is situated in New Register House. The latter has responsibility for many functions, which have in common the recording of information about Scotland's inhabitants, and is thus an institution of vital importance to the genealogist. The fact that these records are kept together is both an advantage and a disadvantage, depending on where in Scotland you live. I have already mentioned ways in which new technological developments such as microfilming have mitigated the consequences of the centralization of Scottish records. Family history archives are no exception, but the most important register from the genealogist's point of view, the post-1855 civil

Register of Births, Marriages and Deaths, is unfortunately only available in Edinburgh. The consolation is that in most cases you will be able quite easily to trace all members of your family who were born, married or died in Scotland after 1855: one day's work to save weeks of probably fruitless searching elsewhere. Other courses of action you might have thought more profitable – such as a visit to your churchyard, local register office or library – come later, when your basic framework from 1855 is established.

Before you go to the General Register Office, it is recommended that you read some background material; it is a good general rule not to visit any institution without having made a preparatory study of its records and organization. Genealogical research is one of the few areas of Scottish local history where there exists an adequate literature. Apart from a free leaflet produced by the General Register Office itself, called the *Ancestry Leaflet*, which you can send for, together with a list of current charges (it costs a few pounds to make a day search), there are three recent monographs, listed in the Further Reading for this chapter.

The main desk where you register is situated in the circular hall, around the walls of which are series of annual volumes marked *births, male and female; marriages, male and female;* and *deaths, male and female*. These are the indexes to the birth, marriage and death certificates, and can be used for a considerable amount of preliminary checking. You will have already collected from your interviews a number of significant dates which can serve as your starting point and you will also want to resolve any discrepancies in your oral evidence. The indexes identify each certificate by means of a code number, and if you want to see the actual document, you fill in a slip with your name and the appropriate reference, and wait to be called and escorted to its cabinet. The certificate provides more information – the names of parents for example, their ages and dates of marriage – so that in turn you can find *their* certificates. By this process you can quickly begin to establish your family tree, and your progress is blocked only when you come up against an individual who left Scotland or who died before 1855, the year in which the civil record began.

It may seem slightly surprising to us that in early times it was not the state which concerned itself with the registration of individuals. The reason seems to be that the individual as such was not seen as a significant entity with interests and rights of his own; he might indeed in some cases have been a slave. Instead it was the church which was responsible, as it was also for the execution of wills, matrimonial matters and slander, all of which have in common a concern for morality and mortality. It was in this context that registration of births, marriages and deaths was seen as an ecclesiastical affair. Several attempts were made by the Church of Scotland to introduce a scheme abetted by the Privy Council, which, in 1616, instructed that each parish should keep 'ane famous book and register' to record baptisms, marriages and deaths. The response was never more than half-hearted, so it is by no means the case that there is a continuous record from that date to 1854. The book was kept by the session clerk or minister of each parish (in some cases, to confuse matters, in the same book as the kirk session minutes), but many were lax or ignorant in their duties, and some books which *were* kept have subsequently been lost. The imposition of a tax on entries did not contribute to good record keeping either. Altogether around 4,000 volumes remain and have been collected together in the General Register Office. Their exploitation in the long term will be made easier by the compilation by the Mormon Church of the International Genealogical Index, an index on microfiche based on parish records and arranged by county. New editions appear as the project proceeds, and it is possible that your local history library will have a copy. Its use will be preferable, for genealogical purposes, to consulting the original parish records, which are also available on microfilm.

Registers of births, marriages and deaths for churches other than the Church of Scotland vary in scale and scope. Quaker files are held by the Scottish Record Office, as are some records of the Methodist and Episcopalian Churches. The Roman Catholic Church maintains its own archive (see page 48) but photocopies of some of its registers are held by the Scottish Record Office. It is essential to remember that the parish registers in the General Register Office only record members of the established church; the frequent schism within the Church of Scotland can cause enormous problems for the family historian. Such difficulties are compounded by the fact that the registers are based on the parish, so that you need to know where your forebears were living. You cannot take it for granted that they remained in one place over a long period, for the view that economic mobility was not a feature of traditional communities is now very much questioned (your own family tree may throw light on the issue).

As we have seen, it was only in the nineteenth century that the state first began to concern itself with the registration of its citizens. The earliest manifestation of this interest was the official census, carried out for the first time in 1801, since which time it has been repeated at ten-year intervals, with the exception of the war year 1941. From 1841 it has consisted of two parts, first the individual returns (from which summary transcriptions were compiled by visiting enumerators – hence the name, enumeration books); and secondly area summaries and statistical analyses. The latter are published immediately after the census is carried out, whilst the enumeration books are supposed to be confidential for 100 years, though the rule has been slightly relaxed (1891 books are open for inspection). In the first four censuses, 1801–31 inclusive, there were no individual returns, only parish summaries. The family researcher will want to concentrate on the enumeration books of 1841–91, of which the 1851 series affords the best harvest, listing all the inhabitants of a house, their status, occupation, and parish of birth. Such records can obviously be used for genealogical purposes, but they also throw light on the composition of households, mobility and economic structure of a community. By collating this data and supplementing it with early photographs and maps, a detailed picture of a street or village (which may not indeed even exist any more) can be obtained. The enumeration books are deposited with the General Register Office, but microfilm copies are for sale and may well be available in your local history library.

For the period after 1891 we must rely on the published census material, which tells us not so much about individuals as about generalized social and economic developments. This is nevertheless valuable material for the local historian. Sociological data such as changing class structure, working patterns and the impact of improvements in health care can be collected, and comparisons between communities can be made – for example between a declining industrial settlement and a prosperous commercial one. How do their inhabitants differ in life expectation, numbers of children, car ownership and other factors?

The quantity of published material has increased from census to census. In the latest, 1981, there are several volumes of tables for each local government region, as well as general information covering Scotland as a whole. This information can be supplemented by that found in other statistical publications, such as the *Scottish Annual Abstract of Statistics*, the *Scottish Health Statistics* and the *Annual Report of the Registrar General for Scotland*. The census data is now held on computer, which means that far more is available than that which appears in book form. Unfortunately for the local historian, some of the printed information is not broken down according to small units, villages, parishes or towns. However, local authorities and health boards need detailed computer print-outs for their administration and planning, and you may be able to gain access to their data. It can be costly to commission a print-out for yourself. Further information on computerized records can be obtained from the Census Customer Services, Ladywell House, Ladywell Road, Edinburgh, EH12 7TF. For the latest census, the most detailed breakdown for populous areas appears in *Census 1981: Key Statistics for Urban Areas, Scotland*.

By this stage you are likely to have been persuaded of the value of registers to the genealogist. Those we have considered so far have been exclusively concerned with the individual; but there are many others which record individuals in the context of specific activities, such as the sale of property, inheritance of land or goods, poor relief, and the making of business contracts, thus relating the person to the social and economic situation in which he lived. Many of these registers are still in current use and will most usually be found in the Scottish Record Office, though published indexes or abridgements are acquired by local history libraries. The Scottish Record Office has produced a family history leaflet (Leaflet Number 9) based upon their use, and a more extensive publication on genealogical sources is in preparation. The registers that deal primarily with property – sasines, valuation rolls and wills – are discussed in more detail in the next chapter; those which concern economic activities, such as the registers of deeds, are looked at in the context of the growth of a settlement, which forms the subject matter of Chapter Six.

Many other historical records obviously do not have their genesis in the requirements of any kind of registration, and genealogical information contained in these is entirely incidental. Their use is liable to cause more frustration, but becomes necessary when òther sources are exhausted. Probably your most sensible course of action when you reach this stage is to take a wider look at your local history library's collections. There may be guidance available in the form of a booklet designed for genealogical researchers. If not, you can get some idea of profitable leads from another library's publication, such as Aberdeen Public Library's *Links in the Chain*, which points to the potential of a wide range of published material. But do not expect that your library will necessarily equal the resources of Aberdeen – the large burgh libraries have older and larger collections than the former county libraries. However, in some cases you may be able to borrow items through the inter-library loan scheme. Failing this, you might consider a visit to your nearest city library. The Scottish Room of the Edinburgh City Library, for example, holds most of the material you might require. It is worth mentioning a few of the most important sources. Parish histories are surprisingly full of references to individuals: many works of this kind are in fact little more than compilations of anecdotes about local 'worthies'. Your local history library may well have indexed them, as well as similar pieces in old newspapers or scrapbooks. Town and county directories have appeared since the middle of the eighteenth century, listing electors, tradesmen and officials; their successors are the electoral registers, telephone directories and community information booklets. Some early directories are listed in an appendix to Gerald Hamilton-Edwards (1983) though this bibliography is far from being comprehensive. Later on, street gazetteers appear, but there is not the comprehensive coverage one finds for England. Your local history library will also hold published works of family history, and will in recent years have received considerable correspondence from family researchers, many of whom will have provided genealogical information. Where this has been of sufficient importance, it may have been retained and filed. Libraries have even been able to put different branches of families in touch with each other.

A final topic to mention in connection with family history is the study of gravestones and their inscriptions, of which there are three aspects – the genealogical, the social and the artistic. All three offer an opportunity for fieldwork. Genealogical recording of grave-stones throughout Scotland has been carried out under the aegis of the Scottish Genealogy Society, 9 Union Street, Edinburgh EH1 3LT, and the findings published in volumes of surveys for different counties. These concentrate on pre-1855 gravestones, understand-ably enough from the genealogical point of view, as subsequent deaths are easily traced through the civil registers. Obviously, if you are wanting to undertake a study of your own, you should contact the Society to ascertain whether you would be duplicating work already carried out; at the same time you can take the opportunity to get advice on how to set about your task. Check with your local history library too, as locally based groups may have been involved in projects of their own. Literature giving background information on technique is listed in the Further Reading section of this chapter.

An interesting project is to compare the results of your fieldwork with surviving burial records and lair plans. Apart from the registers we have been discussing, some burial books and plans have been preserved and are to be found in various locations, amongst heritors' records, church papers, libraries, local registry offices and town and county council archives (in the latter case most often with parish and pre-1975 district council records). Current responsibility lies with the post-1975 district councils. All these sources can be utilized for a related project: the study of attitudes towards death at different times, as revealed for example in the wording of epitaphs. Recording tombstone architecture, on the other hand, demands skills of a different kind, artistic or photographic. The extent of weathering on old stones makes their recording almost an archaeological rescue operation; Victorian stones by contrast are often well preserved and their Gothic fantasies make a fascinating subject for a study.

The process of compiling a family history should ideally be seen merely as a framework within which to find out more about the way our ancestors lived. A list of names, after all, is of little historical interest in itself. One possible approach is to look at these people, not as a collection of independent individuals, but as part of a com-munity, held together by a series of bonds formalized by religious mores, taboos and legal sanctions. One method which relies heavily on the use of the registers we have been looking at, borrowing methodology from anthropological fieldwork, is described in depth in the context of an English parish by Alan MacFarlane (1977). A settlement is seen as a group of partially overlapping communities, based on physical parameters, administrative areas, economic hinterlands and kinship relationships, with various networks (in the mathematical sense where A interacts with B and B with C, but not

A with *C* necessarily) linking members of the settlement to each other in different ways. MacFarlane's has been an ambitious project, covering three hundred years of a parish. For an amateur, even for a local group, this would be impossible, not only because of the time involved but also because it would be difficult in a Scottish context to find a community continuously documented to the required depth.

But the technique can be adapted for smaller projects. The inhabitants are observed in a way analogous to that in which an anthropologist meticulously observes his subjects, working also, usually, in a small self-contained community. Within the period chosen every register is searched, both those we have been considering and others, for example poor rolls, estate rentals and registers of actions in civil and criminal courts. Indeed, each mention of an individual is recorded, and this includes references in the proceedings of local government and church bodies as well as in registers. Information is stored either on index cards or on a home computer, and a similar procedure to that we outlined for family history records is recommended. Separate entries are made out for each appearance of an individual's name, giving details of the transaction, fact or event being recorded. Specific data about properties and other components of the local environment are included, but so also are general subject headings, such as marriages, property sales or business contracts. Various duplicated groupings of cards are then possible (this is where a home computer is an advantage) under different subjects or specific properties, and the juxtaposition of these can suggest new subject headings and further groupings, leading eventually to abstract insights into marriage patterns, for instance, or the varying reactions to criminal behaviour at different times and in different classes of society. The challenge of a social study of this kind is to try to discover how and why customs, morals and religion operate in a community (their real functions are often not the ostensible ones). The difficulty is that we share many bonds with our ancestors and find a problem in looking at them or ourselves with the same detachment and objective criticism as we would a tribe in Africa whose social structures are essentially strange. Our customs and religion too will appear strange from the outside.

Oral history

A natural extension of the oral technique used in family interviews would be a project to find out about the lives of one's relatives and of others who have had similar experiences. Oral history is a particularly twentieth-century development. A tape recorder is not indispensable, although the discipline has obviously flourished since its introduction. Apart from the technical possibilities opened up by this equipment, interest in the subject was also fostered by a shift in the perception of what constituted local history. Paul Thompson (1978) gives the context:

Until the present century, the focus of history was essentially political: a documentation of the struggle for power, in which the lives of ordinary people or the workings of the economy and religion were given little attention. . . . Even local history was concerned with the administration of the . . . parish rather than the day-to-day life of the community and the street. This was partly because historians, who themselves belonged to the administering and governing classes, thought that this was what mattered most. They had developed no interest in the point of view of the labourer, unless he was specifically troublesome; nor – being men – would they have wished to inquire into the changing life experiences of women.

Yet it is almost 'axiomatic', according to the working-class historian Beatrice Webb 'that the mind of the subordinate in any organisation will yield richer deposits of fact than the mind of the principal'.

The literature of the subject includes the early book by Joan Wake (1925) designed for the benefit of groups such as Women's Institutes (it is written mainly with an English parish in mind). In this connection it would be worth considering a group effort, for example with a Scottish Women's Rural Institute branch or a local history society. Some thematic projects too have been undertaken, such as the Scottish Working People's Oral History Project. Literature on methodology and technical aspects is listed in the Further Reading and Information section of this chapter.

Absolutely central to the study of oral history is the School of Scottish Studies, which is part of the University of Edinburgh and situated in George Square, Edinburgh EH8 9LD. It was established in 1951 and was the first institution in Scotland to carry out 'extensive and systematic fieldwork in folklore and regional ethnology'. Tape recording is the principle medium used, and while music and Gaelic culture have figured prominently in its programmes, attention has also been paid to farming life, social customs, crafts and living conditions.

The recorded tapes at the School are extensively indexed, a point of crucial importance. In your family history study you may well have encountered a relative who tended to ramble: consider that this problem will be ten times worse on a tape in which every irrelevant digression will be recorded without even the consolation of your being able to skim quickly through your material (as you could with notes) to find the passage you are looking for. Obviously you cannot control your subject in oral recording, and indeed it can be restricting and counter-productive to over-organize the interview (the interviewee will not relax). But what you must be able to do is to extract from what you have recorded the information you need at any juncture and to rearrange and index it under the headings you have chosen. The staff at the School of Scottish Studies will be able to give you advice on these matters. In the case of their own collections, an inventory sheet is prepared for each tape, detailing the subjects discussed and approximate position on the tape. This is not enough in itself: a subject index must also be prepared, preferably on cards, bringing together subjects discussed on different tapes. The subject classification scheme used by the School of Scottish Studies for this purpose will be eminently suitable for your project too.

In oral recording, as with your interviews with relatives for family history research, it is essential to have a structured list of questions against which to match what you are being told, and a considerable amount of thought needs to be given to this before you venture on your first interview. You will also require what are known as prompts, to jog the memory when an interviewee threatens to dry up. If for example the subject of farm machinery is to be investigated, you yourself will need to research the subject so that relevant material can be naturally introduced.

Oral history recording is obviously an art, and there are pitfalls. Some of the information gathered can be trivial, and there is a tendency to believe what you are told, or to treat your subject with awe. Nor can one expect interviewees to become shining examples of impartiality and clarity when presented with a tape recorder. They are not historians; it is wrong to expect them to be so. Their shortcomings indeed are likely to be exaggerated by the interview situation, in which both memory and vanity are likely to play tricks. As a safeguard, each interview must be checked for internal consistency, cross-checked with non-oral sources and finally placed in a wider context, for example your own background reading or your knowledge of the individual concerned. Remember in this respect that you too can distort the truth by interposing your own preconceptions, by the use of leading questions and insinuations. Neither your opinions, nor those of your subject, are necessarily very relevant. Some people tend to agree with what is suggested to them; but you must not argue with those who do not; rather you must gently lead them back to the ground you want to cover. A skilful interviewing technique is called for such as you may see in the best investigative television programmes – not mind you, that of the political interviewer, this is a different sort of game altogether. You can learn instead from the confidant who knows when to speak and when to leave just that extra second or two of silence which can provoke the unexpected confidence. Another common pitfall of oral history is sentimentality, the 'good old days' syndrome. Such attitudes, especially among the elderly, are often not a realistic reflection of how they actually felt at the time. Sentimentality can be a self-defence against unpleasant memories, and the view that one has of the past tends to be coloured by many psychological factors; it is part of the interviewer's skill so to trigger the memory that forgotten feelings are revived. The key to success is sympathy allied to critical scepticism, alert to the generalizing tendency to which sentimentality is prone.

Once you have made your recordings, there comes the problem of what to do with them. The tapes themselves you may want to deposit with the School of Scottish Studies or your local library for use by others – that is your contribution to the source materials of future historians. But before you do that, it is advantageous to prepare some published work – after all, your tapes are not widely accessible, nor have they been edited to afford easy exploitation. Publishing can take three forms: a single life narrative, a collection of stories linked by a common theme or locality, or an analytical account, abstracted from the mass of material and presented in your own words as opposed to those of the interviewees. The School of Scottish Studies' journal *Tocher* adopts the first approach, whilst its *Scottish Studies* uses the third. A famous example of the second is Ronald Blythe's *Akenfield*, Allen Lane, 1969.

Transcribing your tapes into written form presents certain problems, as normal speech is surprisingly full of hesitations, grunts, repetitions and the like. These may have subtle connotations which modify expression, but to transcribe them literally makes for an unreadable text. Similarly speech, when reproduced in writing, has an odd habit of appearing like rather bad poetry in free verse style – the sentences for example are shorter than in written prose. This can give a misleading, sentimental complexion on the page, which may not reflect at all the mood of the informant. The insertion of some written grammar and linking clauses will avoid this problem, though great care must be taken not to affect or distort the meaning. It is only fair to add that this view may be anathema to some purists; but their argument is dubious in that the very act of transferring one medium – speech – to another – writing – creates distortions in itself.

A *Register of Oral History Tapes* is maintained by the Scottish Record Office, based on data supplied from various institutions. The *Annual Report of the Keeper of the Records of Scotland 1982* discusses the material. Currently in preparation is the *British Library National Sound Archive Directory of Recorded Sound Resources in the United Kingdom*.

Finally, a reminder about technical standards is apposite. However good your preparation as an historian, your project can be ruined by poor technical work. The size of room used, relative placing of microphone and recorder and the surface on which equipment is placed all affect the quality of the recordings, and expert advice is essential if mistakes are to be avoided.

Labour history

In your genealogical researches, you will frequently have encountered information about the occupations of your ancestors (given for example in registers of births, marriages and deaths, in census enumeration books and in some valuation rolls). The context can be widened by investigating employment conditions which, in the nineteenth century in particular, were the subject of numerous royal commissions. The 1816 *Report of a Select Committee on Children employed in the Manufactories of the United Kingdom*, the 1834 *Report of the Select Committee on Handloom Weavers*, the 1831–2 *Report of the Select Committee on Children in Mills and Factories*, the 1838 *Report of the Committee on Combinations of Workmen*, and the 1871 *Report of the Royal Commission on the Truck System* (a system which obliged employees to spend their wages in shops run by the employers) are but a few of the major sources. You may be inclined to think of government commissions as bland uninteresting publications, but this was not the case in the nineteenth century. As one social historian, Thomas Ferguson (1958) has said:

> The outspoken comment of other days, often freely expressed by civil servants of varying seniority, has long been replaced by the official anonymity of our times; gone are the forthright expressions of opinion which used to be accepted as a matter of course, but would now be regarded as political dynamite, certain to embarrass the minister.

In the course of their work the commissioners heard representations from all parts of the country, which were published as evidence along with the recommendations. Your local history library may have relevant sections, whilst the entire reports are more likely to be found in university libraries and the National Library of Scotland, whence they can sometimes be borrowed through the inter-library loan scheme. All you need to do is to make the request at your local library. Sources of information about government commissions are given on page 41. Another useful official source originates from the responsibility of the sheriff courts from 1895 for the conduct of fatal accident enquiries – of course many accidents happened in the workplace. The wealth of information in private papers (of companies, estates and employers' organizations) is illustrated by a Scottish Record Office publication, *The Coalminers*, 1983. From the employees' side there are trade union and trades council records, which are well represented in the National Library of Scotland's collections.

In the case of your eighteenth-century ancestors, employment was unlikely to have been in industry, the factory system only developing in a substantial way at the start of the nineteenth century. They may perhaps have been miners, but agriculture or trade would have accounted for the majority. Conditions of farm work were themselves the subject of government commissions; three for example date from the second half of the nineteenth century alone. The Highlands were a perennial problem: the Scottish Record Office contains the *Accounts, correspondence and other papers relative to the proceedings taken for relief of destitution in the Highlands 1837–50* (*Destitution Papers* for short) and also the *Papers of the Society formed to aid emigration from the Western Highlands and Islands to the British Colonies after 1851.* These and other records are included in the source list on the Highlands (Source List 26), whilst a related topic, crofting disturbances, has warranted a separate list. In 1884 appeared the famous *Napier Report* (*the Royal Commission on the Conditions of the Crofters and Cottars in the Highlands and Islands of Scotland*). Farming records are dealt with in more detail on pages 125–7.

If your ancestors were tradesmen, they will probably have been members of a trades incorporation if they lived in a burgh, where, from medieval times, both manufacturing and retailing (through markets and fairs) were quite rigidly regulated – free enterprise as we understand it was quite unknown. In most periods the merchant guild was the dominant force, but the incorporations of craftsmen exerted some influence to the extent of securing positions within the town council, their representatives being known as 'deacons'. Democracy of course was also unknown. Minute books of the old town councils and incorporations will therefore be a fund of information, the latter in particular in that they served at the one time as trade unions, business cartels and friendly societies. The last mentioned also existed as specially constituted bodies with the function of providing social security to their members. The Scottish Record Office has a good collection of their records, whilst published rules and articles are often found in local history library collections.

Schooling

At the time of the Reformation in 1560 most burghs of reasonable size boasted a grammar school. These had originally been church schools, but the burghs had gradually assumed responsibility for their upkeep, whereby they began to claim right of patronage too. The Reformation established the following educational structure: elementary schools in rural parishes (for ages roughly five to eight); grammar schools in burghs (for all the town children of any age and for the rural children aged eight to twelve). This was the theory; in practice little was implemented, which led to the setting up of a church commission in 1627 to report on the educational state of the parishes. Records for 49 parishes have survived (see page 51). The 1696 Act of Settling Schools reaffirmed the principle of providing schools in every parish. Under this scheme the heritors were to pay the salary and maintain the school building, while the kirk session was to undertake the day-to-day running, a situation which remained unchanged in general terms until the mid-nineteenth century. In researching this period therefore the approach will depend upon whether the school in question was a burgh or rural school. For burgh schools (known incidentally by a wide variety of names, burgh, grammar and, for older children, high school) the council minutes will be a primary source; for the rural parish schools one must turn to the minute books of heritors and records of the kirk sessions.

Alongside the church schools there also grew up a large number of private and endowed educational establishments. Examples are those planted by the Scottish Society for the Propagation of Christian Knowledge after 1709, mainly in the Highlands, and middle-class academies, which flourished from the mid-eighteenth century in the larger burghs. Industrial schools were to be found in several Scottish towns by 1850 and originated in an effort to suppress child beggars. An Act of 1854 empowered the courts to commit vagrant children to these schools, which were subsequently called approved schools. Records of the trusts which were responsible·for endowed institutions have sometimes survived, and recourse can also be made to Court of Session papers, the court governing the administration of trust law.

The nineteenth century brought a crisis to the educational system. The rapid growth of industrial towns in previously rural areas and the demands for new kinds of learning (more secular subjects and less Latin) put strains upon the existing facilities. Burgh schools widened their curricula (you may read of 'English' schools, 'mathematical' schools and so on – these were all part of the burgh school system). Extra parish schools, known as 'side schools' (in *quoad sacra* parishes 'parliamentary' or 'sessional' schools) were set up. In 1832 the first government grant scheme was introduced, with the attendant school inspection (the records of which are held with Scottish Education Department files). The Royal Commission on Education (the Argyll Commission) reported between 1865 and 1867, the outcome being a complete restructuring of the educational framework, set out in the 1872 Education (Scotland) Act. School boards were set up in each district – co-extensive with the burghs in urban areas and based upon the parishes elsewhere. The members were elected on a limited franchise. The records of the school boards are an invaluable source, and are usually held with the relevant county council records. The Act also established a central department, the Scotch Education Department, whose files, together with those of its successor, the Scottish Education Department, are to be found in the Scottish Record Office. Another important commission from this period, the Endowed Institutions Commission of 1878, looked at the wide range of charitable schools. The school boards lasted only to 1918; it was felt that the areas they covered were too small, and new education authorities were instituted, co-extensive with the county council areas (though not part of county councils). This new system was in operation only up to 1929, when the education authorities *were* incorporated into the county councils, comprising education committees within those bodies. Another innovation of 1918, introduced to compensate for the loss of local control, was the school management committee drawn from parents and teachers – the precursor of area education subcommittees, parent–teacher associations and the current schools councils. Responsibility for education passed to the regional councils in 1975.

In researching the period since 1872 perhaps the most valuable source will be the school log book. Its whereabouts can vary: it may be still in the school, with the county council records, with the district council or in the Scottish Record Office. In any case, you are best advised to start your enquiries with the school, which may have other materials such as photographs and copies of old school magazines. Speech day reports from local newspapers can also be fruitful.

Social welfare

The importance of the church in the affairs of the individual and the community has been noted on more than one occasion. In the provision of social welfare – poor relief, health services and hospitals – we find a similar situation. In medieval times these functions were carried out by the hospitals or hospices maintained by monastic institutions, where the poor, the sick and travellers found accommodation (their locations are sometimes commemorated in the common place name 'spittal'). As for the state, the Scottish Parliament and Privy Council made frequent pronouncements on the problems of beggars and lepers, motivated not so much by charity as concern for the stability of society. Information will also be found in the minutes of town councils, who discovered (as happens today in third world countries) that the unemployed poor gravitated to the burghs, where they threatened to become both a burden on poor relief funds and a potential source of disorder. You might be interested in a comparative study of solutions sought in the past and today, or you could broaden the study to an investigation of the outsider or dispossessed in Scottish history. Gipsies are one group whom you can trace through eighteenth-century justice of the peace records to recent county council and district council minutes books.

In such a project, as in the study of welfare generally, a fault to watch out for is the application of today's standards to the issues of the past, either as a glib reference to former barbarities, for instance, or in the context of a full-scale polemical diatribe. Take the following situation described by Thomas Ferguson (1948), in which the subject is epidemic in the seventeenth century:

> Under pain of death the master of the house in which any person fell sick had to report the case immediately to visitors or searchers.

The death penalty was often exacted, as it was with an Edinburgh tailor who was brought to execution 'on a gibbet before his own door' for having failed to report the illness of his wife who died of the disease; but, the rope having broken 'at the will of God he eschapit' and was banished the city forever. Women offenders were drowned.

A social historian who opposes the death penalty might see in this passage an opportunity to denounce the inhumanity of town councils of the day. A feminist likewise might take exception to the different death penalty meted out to women. But both these reactions would be inappropriate: the fear of disease in an age before medical advances made us more confident in our ability to handle our environment would have led to quite different social standards. Our own religion, politics and morals have no relevance. Indeed the historian must strip away his personal predilections one by one as his studies show him how they have come to be formed – through the processes of social history, not of individual will. We can certainly take account of our own viewpoints; in fact the most perceptive historians will use them as a springboard to formulate questions about themselves and how they differ from their forebears. But the object will be to understand, not to judge. Raiding the past for polemical ammunition is valid, just possibly, as an activity for those who want to change present conditions, but such practices should not be confused with historical study.

A project which ties in neatly with the above discussion is to trace the genesis of current social concerns: it has been argued for example that compassion for the poor was a Victorian invention – poor law records from the eighteenth and nineteenth centuries could be used to investigate the claim, together with the records of charitable institutions (GD).

Religious hospitals were largely abandoned at the Reformation, and the heritors and the kirk sessions came to bear the main burden of poor relief, attempts being made to solve the problem of beggars by requiring paupers to remain in their own parishes. In landward areas poor relief was paid out more often than not at the church door (though local taxes could be levied) and kirk session minutes provide details of recipients and monies paid. In the burghs poor rolls were maintained by the town councils, relief usually being distributed by the magistrates. Here poorhouses were sometimes built, though outdoor relief was the more usual system (i.e. the poor were paid 'social security' and remained in their homes).

Church administration lasted until the middle of the nineteenth century – it broke down under the pressures of rapid industrialization. The problems were analysed in two major reports, those of the Committee of the General Assembly on the Management of the Poor in Scotland (1839) and of the Royal Commission on the Poor Laws (1844). The latter led to the introduction of a new civil system of poor relief, administered by new bodies known as parochial boards based upon traditional parish areas. These were superseded by elected parish councils in 1894, which in turn were replaced by district councils in 1929. District councils were abolished in 1974. The parochial boards established poorhouses more widely than before (often in 'combination') and the day books or log books of these institutions can provide the background to an interesting study. They can be used in conjunction with plans of the poorhouses (several are held by the National Monuments Record of Scotland). The minute books of parochial boards are also extremely valuable sources: the social background of applicants is often investigated in detail, especially when – as frequently happened – the board members attempted to pass off responsibility for relief on to neighbouring parishes whence the applicant had come. You might be able to trace the individual biographies of many of the destitute as they passed from one parish to the next in search of casual farm work, and you might find them too in the poorhouses' log books. The replacement of parochial boards with parish councils was partly motivated by the fact that the system did not operate with complete success, a state of affairs which was reflected in the appointment of further committees of enquiry – the Select Committee on the Poor Laws in Scotland (1868–9) and the Royal Commission on the Poor Laws and Relief of Distress (Scottish report 1909). The changes of attitude and approach that resulted from the establishment of parish councils could be made the subject of a comparative study.

The overseeing of parochial boards and their successors was the responsibility of a General Board of Supervision (1845–93), followed by the Local Government Board for Scotland. The annual reports of both bodies will be useful to the researcher. In 1919 the Scottish Board of Health replaced the Local Government Board and in turn became the Department of Health for Scotland in 1929.

Health and hospital services also originated with the medieval hospices, early periods being dominated by the fear of the great epidemics of leprosy, typhus, cholera and smallpox. Leper hospitals were a feature of early burghs. Hospitals as we understand them began to appear in the seventeenth century, though it was only gradually that a distinction came to be made between an infirmary for the sick and an epidemic hospital. Early infirmaries were charitable foundations, though town councils and trade incorporations sometimes shared financing. These hospitals formed the backbone of the system right up to 1948. Their records are held in some cases by the Scottish Record Office (inventory HH); others are being deposited in medical archive centres established by the health boards, in Greater Glasgow, Grampian, Dumfries, Lothian and Fife for example. Local boards of health, sometimes called fever commissions, appeared in the early nineteenth century in response to epidemics, such as the devastating cholera outbreak of 1832. These were temporary bodies, but from the middle of the century views on the importance of health and sanitation and the relation between the two were vigorously prosecuted. The famous *Report of the Poor Law Commissioners into the Sanitary Conditions of the Labouring Population of Great Britain*, 1842 led to various measures – powers for police commissioners in burghs and parochial boards in rural areas, and subsequently to the first major piece of legislation, the Public Health (Scotland) Act 1867.

Meantime, medical services had improved also. Parochial medical officers of health had been attached to the parochial boards at an early stage (these were GPs acting in an advisory capacity). The first full-time officers were appointed in Glasgow and Edinburgh in the 1860s, whilst county medical officers of health were appointed in 1889, to work in tandem with sanitation officers. The annual reports of both officials are full of useful material; they are to be found in the Scottish Record Office HH archives and also in health board archive centres. The supervision boards already mentioned in connection with poor relief were similarly responsible for health matters. The appreciation of special problems in the Highlands led to the establishment of the Highlands and Islands Medical Services Committee (1912–28).

The poorhouses, both before and after the setting up of the parochial boards, had served in a limited way as hospitals for the poorest members of society. In towns, they were progressively converted into full-time hospitals, and this trend became general after the Local Government (Scotland) Act 1929. During the same period small nursing homes and cottage hospitals appeared; these were charitable institutions, subscribed to and patronized by the better-off in society.

This chapter has shown a repeating pattern of the transfer of functions from church to civil authorities in the nineteenth century. In the sphere of social welfare, our own century has seen a new trend – from a local to a central government responsibility. Provision of poor relief was transferred piecemeal up to the passing of the National Assistance Act of 1948, when all local government involvement ended and hospital services were taken over by the state under the National Health (Scotland) Act 1947. Local authorities remain in charge of social work and related services and of preventive medicine and environmental health.

For any period over the last century a study could be made of the services offered in the different types of hospital, or of the social background of the patients. The different registers looked at in this chapter allow the researcher to amass a meaningful amount of information about any individual at all in terms of his social status and employment. You could make your project a detailed analysis of all patients in local hospitals on any one day. A wider study would be to assess the impact of epidemics on the community, not only in relation to the immediate disruption to daily life but also in the longer-term formation of attitudes and beliefs. The growth of health resorts is an interesting topic: only later did holidays take on the recreational connotations we associate with them today. A study of causes of mortality can be made by using the registers of deaths for any period from the seventeenth century. Researchers with more specialized knowledge could tackle the development of medicine, surgical techniques or patient care. The treatment of insanity can be a fascinating study, either medical or social, and there is a variety of material available. By the end of the eighteenth century there was still no separate provision, but an act to regulate 'madhouses' was passed in 1815 – they were to be licensed and inspected by sheriff court officials together with medical representatives. The *Report of the Royal Commission on Lunacy*, 1855 led to the formation of district asylums controlled by district lunacy boards, whose minute books, engrossed with county council archives, can be consulted. Census enumeration books list asylums as a separate item at the end of the section for each parish and give details about inmates.

Sociological studies

The local historian should feel at liberty to raid other disciplines for ideas that appear promising – a procedure which we have seen used by MacFarlane in his anthropological analysis of a historical settlement. The sister discipline of sociology should also prove fruitful in community studies, and it has even been suggested by Peter Worsley (1970) that 'the best history is in fact sociological: the sociology of the past'. Where there is a common methodology (in our case a focus on the individual and particular rather than the general) and shared aims (the understanding of social structures and interactions) there is an increased likelihood that conceptual approaches and terminology developed in one discipline will also be found useful in the other.

Social stratification, by age, sex and class, is a common theme of the sociologist. An interesting study for the local historian might be to compare the status of women or children at various times. An established methodology also exists for the analysis of differences between rural and urban communities. The former, it is claimed, consist mainly of primary groups – family, church, etc. – whereas in urban areas secondary groups, based on common social and political interests, weaken the traditional bonds. You might like to examine this thesis through a comparative study of communities. The mid nineteenth century will be a suitable period, as the presence of local newspapers will allow you easily to monitor the growth of secondary institutions. Newspapers can also be used in a study of how national events impinge on a locality. What for example is the emotional reaction to war? Do we find a change in the tone of the newspaper, a need for an aggressive propaganda, perhaps, or for a comforting sentimentality?

A precise terminology is available for the study of culture, understood in its widest sense to include institutions such as the family as well as the artefacts and belief systems of the group. Even in a traditional rural culture, there can be rich variety, and elements which might be thought to be purely functional can prove to be unexpectedly subtle. An example is the horse-drawn threshing mills in the east of Scotland, where the persistence of a complex (and expensive) conical roofing style had no functional justification.

Group theory attempts to understand how individuals react with one another and how institutions control or formalize individual impulses, the operation of which process could be illustrated by a study of the early eighteenth century, when private jurisdictions were giving way to collective county institutions such as justices of the peace and commissioners of supply – allegiance to the state rather than to one's kin only became widespread in Scotland in the eighteenth century. Within these institutions you might like to examine the ways in which decisions were reached, using techniques such as game theory. The local historian is at a disadvantage in that he cannot sit in at the meetings or interview the protagonists as a sociologist could – to compensate, it will be necessary to choose periods for which background information about policy making and power struggles will be available. A related study would be to look at the maintenance of prestige within the community. In the eighteenth century there was considerable overlap among economic, religious and political peer groups which resulted in a clearly defined social hierarchy. Its dissolution in the nineteenth century could be monitored through an analysis of the compositions of institutions. One could study too the reaction of a group whose status is under threat – in the letters its members wrote to the newspapers for example. A thesis which could be pursued is that threats to the dominant position of a group would lead to a renewed emphasis on the rituals and symbols of its authority.

If you live in the Highlands a topic which might appeal to you is the study of local clans and the factors which encouraged the survival of this form of social organization. The system crystallized from the attitudes mentioned above – allegiance to kinsmen rather than to the state or a locality. Clan organization was possibly strengthened by the practice of 'manrent', whereby a minor laird bound himself to serve an earl or lord (in the later Middle Ages a titled nobility supplanted the feudal baronial system whereby men were bound to the land rather than an individual). Many of these bonds of manrent survive in family muniments, and transcriptions have been published in J. Wormald (1985). In conjunction with manrent went the 'blood-feud' – an organized system of private justice by the kin group based on the principle of material compensation in contrast to the rising system of the 'upstart' lawyers and their courts, based on state-sanctioned retribution. Clans were similar in some ways to the modern Mafia (though not invariably persecuted by the state) and you could make a comparative study of the two systems.

Studying clans is not easy – records are scarce and witnesses uninformed, a shortcoming which afflicts much of the current secondary literature too. Records you could look at include bonds of manrent, the Acts of the Commission for Keeping Order in the Highlands and Islands 1587–1602 (among Privy Council records), early justice of the peace archives, the four volumes of *Highland Papers* published by the Scottish History Society, travellers' accounts and Forfeited Estate Papers. Nineteenth-century enquiries into grievances in relation to the clearances are useful for an understanding of the Highlanders' concept of relationship with the chief.

Finally a potential project for the ambitious local historian would be to bring together many of the ideas pursued in this chapter in the compilation of a full-scale biography of a community. It would need to be a small community, and the period covered would need to be fairly short and to post-date the newspaper era. No better model could be found for such a study than the French historian Emmanuel le Roy Ladurie's *Montaillou*, Scolar Press, 1978, a detailed biography of a French village between the years 1294 and 1324.

Chapter Five

BUILDINGS PAST AND PRESENT

The last chapter was concerned with an investigation of the people of history; this concentrates on the material remains they have left behind, the buildings and artefacts of the local landscape. Just as there is one institution – the General Register Office – concerned with records of individuals, so there is another exclusively committed to the study of buildings – the Royal Commission on the Ancient and Historical Monuments of Scotland, located at 54 Melville Street, Edinburgh EH3 7HF (telephone: 031 225 5994), to which is attached the National Monuments Record of Scotland (formerly the Scottish National Building Record), 7 Coates Place, Edinburgh EH3 7AA.

The Royal Commission is the older body. It differs from the royal commissions we have studied hitherto in being a standing or permanent body, and has been responsible for producing a series of volumes, known as inventories, of all noteworthy historic and prehistoric monuments. This immense survey programme began at the beginning of the century and is still only half finished, the inventories being compiled county by county and published as each is completed, in which event the volume or volumes for your area will be available through your local library. A list of those published to date appears in the Royal Commission's leaflet *Recording Scotland's Heritage*, which also gives details of summary lists of noted monuments (without descriptive detail) published since 1977. The Royal Commission is also responsible for the National Archaeological Survey, consisting among other things of a systematic aerial photographic survey of the country. Aerial photographs provide an enormous amount of information about archaeological sites, extending our understanding of those which are known and revealing many that were previously unknown. Owing to the disruption to soil drainage caused by man's activities in farming and building, a permanent alteration is effected in the landscape which can become graphically illustrated in variant crop growth – hence the expression 'crop mark' – and which can be detected from above when the light is falling at a suitable angle. Differential rates of drainage of snow can also produce dramatic marks.

The National Monuments Record was originally set up in 1941 'to make and preserve records of historically important buildings in anticipation of their possible destruction by enemy action'. Since its amalgamation with the Royal Commission, its concern has been with both historic and prehistoric sites; and it is organized, accordingly, into architectural and archaeological sections, a distinction which reflects methodological differences in the study of historic and prehistoric settlements. The science of archaeology developed principally to provide knowledge of those periods for which there was no historical (i.e. written) record, but its initial weakness was to attempt to compensate for this absence by trying to provide equivalent information from alternative sources. However, the areas which historical records are eminently suited to explore are those concerned with men's motives and actions – politics, governments, wars, invasions – for all of which the study of material remains does not readily yield data. Wars and invasions in particular at one time dominated archaeological debate but today archaeologists tend to argue that they cannot say anything useful on these subjects, however much the remaining evidence is manipulated to that end. Instead they claim that the strenth of archaeology lies rather in its ability to give an integrated interpretation of a landscape, and to describe the environmental system in which a community operated, and how the different elements in that system – geography, agriculture and trade for example – interrelate. In short, it can deal with everything relating to man's interaction with his environment, which leaves material remains in the landscape, as opposed to his relationships with other human groups, which do not. This approach is called *analytical archaeology*, and it consitutes an exciting challenge to the local historian in that he too is concerned to piece together a detailed reconstruction from a focusing on the processes at work in a geographically limited area. By its use he can throw light on those periods of his settlement's history which hitherto have not been satisfactorily explored (we have already mentioned the fact that from the point of view of local communities, Scotland is in some respects prehistoric even into the sixteenth century).

Prehistoric studies

The simplest and most popular form of archaeology is treasure hunting with a metal detector. This said, historians are agreed that it is a potentially destructive occupation, which actually militates against the growth of our knowledge of the past. This is because the treasure hunter tends not to understand that the context in which an object is found can tell us more about the society which made it than the object itself. Nowadays the use of metal detectors is forbidden on known archaeological sites. If you have used or do use a metal detector, try and find out about a current archaeological dig near your home and ask to go along and see what is going on. It may seem rather dull compared with your own adventures, but consider that though the detail which is being carefully recorded in itself may seem trivial, it serves to build up a meticulous picture without which it would be impossible to say anything about the way the community was functioning. The objects which you find with your metal detector by contrast are totally divorced from the essential significance which objects have for the historian, in terms of their use, the time at which they were used and the total array of technology of which they formed a part.

For those who are interested and can feel the excitement and intellectual stimulus of archaeological excavation (the archaeologist is akin to a detective in a crime novel, piecing together a solution from fragmentary materials), the central body to contact is the Council for British Archaeology Scottish Regional Group, c/o National Museum of Antiquities, Queen Street, Edinburgh EH2 1JD. Others who might be involved in projects include your local antiquarian or local history society, universities' departments of archaeology and sometimes their extra-mural departments also. Organizing an excavation is no work for an amateur: this is one area in which you would destroy far more than you discover. But under the right guidance you can become a proficient field worker.

If you want to find background information about archaeological sites, try first the proceedings or transactions of your local antiquarian society. Then check the indexes to the *Proceedings of the Society of Antiquaries of Scotland* (your local history library should have these) which will quickly tell you of any articles or notices about specific sites. The Society of Antiquaries of Scotland, c/o the National Museum of Antiquities, has for over a century been in the forefront of Scottish archaeological studies. Excavations themselves are listed in the annual volumes of *Discovery and Excavation in Scotland: an annual survey of Scottish archaeological discoveries, excavations, surveys and publications*, published by the Council for British Archaeology Scottish Regional Group, which again you should find in your local history library. The same body also publishes the journal *Scottish Archaeological Forum*. Unfortunately there is no publication which tells you the whereabouts of the artefacts and on-site reports and drawings. So unless published material has appeared in one of the journals mentioned, you may have to make a few enquiries to ascertain these details. A useful starting point will be the Ancient Monuments Division of the Scottish Development Department, 3/11 Melville Street, Edinburgh EH3 7PE (telephone 031 226 2570), where you can also find out whether a particular site has ever been excavated. For those monuments owned by the Department itself (in its custodial role for the Department of the Environment) leaflets are sometimes available. Other information on sites, including comprehensive bibliographical references, can be found on the topographical sheets compiled originally by the Archaeological Branch of the Ordnance Survey, which was responsible for the mapping of archaeological sites on Ordnance Survey maps. In 1983 it was disbanded and its work taken over by the National

Monuments Record, the topographical sheets being transferred at the same time. It is quite possible that your local history library will have photocopies of the sheets of local relevance. Arrangement is according to National Grid Reference (the same applies to most other archaeological records), so if you are paying a visit or phoning, make a note of the references in advance (instructions on their formulation are given on Ordnance Survey maps). You will also want to consult the Royal Commission on the Ancient and Historical Monuments of Scotland's aerial photographs of archaeological sites; these too you will find at the National Monuments Record. They may tell you of recently discovered sites not mentioned in maps and parish histories. The interpretation of aerial photographs is discussed on page 117.

The use of archaeological data involves complex skills, and it is only in the last few years that many excavations have been conducted in the detail required for analytical work. Of course the local historian is quite dependent upon the archaeologist to ask the kind of question of his material to which he wants an answer. This said, however, there are general environmental factors that we can establish ourselves, for example soil, climate and prehistoric farming methods, which we can exploit to propose tentative interpretations of the workings of the community involved. This subject is dealt with further in the next chapter.

Though the driving impulse behind the archaeological revolution of the nineteenth century was the desire to learn about prehistory, the science of archaeology is not confined to antiquity, and can be defined as the study of the past through the impact of man's activities on his physical environment. In researching historical periods, it can be most fruitfully used in juxtaposition with written records, to provide insights which neither alone could give. Modern hybrid disciplines such as historical geography owe much to the combined use of physical and written records. By the same token prehistoric studies can be enhanced: for example information about social and economic forces derived from written sources can be used to posit developments in prehistoric communities where the environmental conditions of the settlements appear similar across a range of cultural factors. The changes in the economy of a settlement as expressed by different finds and different organizational patterns at two site levels of an excavation can thus be explored. Our definition of archaeology also makes clear the breadth of archaeological activity, which is wider than the specialized field of excavation. All kinds of fieldwork may be regarded as aspects of the subject, including the recording of churchyards which we discussed in the last chapter and the recording of buildings and industrial sites which is looked at in the next section. In this area too we are looking for an effective combination of written and archaeological information.

Studying houses

We have suggested that the appeal of family history lies in the immediate way in which it links our own lives with those of our forebears, thereby stimulating that curiosity about time and change which is a hallmark of the historian. Another very immediate area in which these same personal emotions can be triggered is the study of one's own house.

As with family history, some of the source material is lying all around you, for example your title deed, of which you will either have a copy or be able to obtain one from your solicitor or building society. The legal terminology is perhaps difficult to understand, so it will pay you to study relevant textbooks of Scottish law, some of which are mentioned in the Further Reading and Information section of Chapter Three (such knowledge will of course also be very useful in the study of registers, charters and other legal documents). Your title deeds may tell you from whom you bought the house and hopefully also about some previous transactions involving the site. It may tell you when the house was built, but this is unlikely to be the case for older property. This is because such a house would probably have been part of an estate or terrace, and a property deed would not be drawn up until it was sold off as an independent unit (the 'founding charter' will usually be recorded in your deeds). For those of you in council or privately rented accommodation, your title deeds will be in the hands of the proprietor.

The study of your house offers at an early stage the opportunity for a piece of fieldwork – the recording of its fabric. R. W. McDowell, *Recording Old Houses: a Guide*, Council for British Archaeology, 1980 and R. W. Brunskill, *Illustrated Handbook of Vernacular Architecture*, 2nd edition, Faber, 1978 are basic guides to setting about the task and identifying different structural elements. Features about which you can make notes include the stone or brick employed, the roof construction, the joints used and the layout of rooms. Look carefully for signs of alterations, and for changes in style or materials used. Measure up the rooms and make a plan of the whole house as it is now, then try and work out from any anomalies you have discovered how it may have looked formerly, producing further plans accordingly. Go and see anybody who remembers your house – family, friends and others – before you went to live there. Ask them questions, using the oral techniques we discussed in connection with family history research. If your house is part of a group, go and see your neighbours and have a look round their houses to see whether they are the same. If there are quite a few of them, you will be able at a later stage to construct a fascinating little study on how they have changed, and more importantly, why they have changed as they have. You could for example compare the sizes of families in the houses over the last century and the occupations of the tenants to see if you can detect a general pattern that correlates with the kinds of alterations made. As well as friends and neighbours, contact any old masons or joiners who are knowledgeable about former methods of building construction: their technical understanding will reveal more than you would ever find out on your own. An architect too may be able to provide an original insight.

This survey technique can be extended in various ways. You might be interested generally in styles of architecture or different building methods and can make a study of houses in your area accordingly. Building styles sometimes evolved, as we mentioned in the last chapter, for other than functional reasons, and you might like to trace the history of particular features and try to relate them to the aspirations of different social groups. Another project would be to locate old quarries and brickworks on early Ordnance Survey maps and to discover where the materials were used. A whole area could be mapped in this way for different periods of history, and the study could be linked to the economic history of the enterprises involved. If you have skills in art, you could undertake a project to record buildings by means of detailed drawings or photographs. A group would be able to harness the different skills of its members in such a study, which need not be confined to houses: it can be extended to administrative, commercial and industrial buildings – farmyards, factories or railways – in which emphasis can be less on the architecture and more on functional and engineering analysis.

If you are contemplating such a project, it will be as well to do some initial research as to what has already been surveyed, for unless you are contributing original source material to the historical record, the rationale of fieldwork is considerably undermined. In other words it is pointless to duplicate work that has already been done. In respect of industrial archaeology for example, it has been pointed out by Philip Riden (1983) that from the middle of the nineteenth century Ordnance Survey maps have been produced to the scale of 50 inches to the mile for urban areas, and 25 inches to the mile for other inhabited areas. A reproduction of the ground plan of a factory, for instance, would involve the expenditure of a large amount of effort, which could all be avoided if you telephoned your local history library and asked for a photocopy of the area concerned. Similarly for the more detailed drawing and photographing of elevations, the National Monuments Record may have existing surveys (they hold for example the industrial archaeology files compiled by Strathclyde University); and in the case of engineering drawings of specific on-site features, there may be detailed drawings among patent records (see pp. 133–4).

Property registers

At this stage in the study of your house, you will hopefully be in a position to demonstrate to yourself the value of having historical records to throw your archaeological discoveries into sharp relief. In this endeavour, we can begin, as we did for family history research, with series of registers, which in the case of properties have been continuously maintained from the seventeenth century and before.

During the Middle Ages there spread across Europe the custom of preserving, by means of documents called 'instruments', the evidence of transactions between parties. The person responsible for drawing up the instrument was known as a notary; hence the transactions were known as 'notarial instruments'. Notaries operated privately though sometimes in association with town councils, the instruments being entered in 'protocol books'. Property transactions form an important part of these records.

At this juncture we should make clear the distinction in Scots law between heritable property (also called heritage) and moveable property. The former includes all objects naturally immoveable, such as land and mineral resources, or fixed to the ground, such as buildings. The property is called heritable because until recently it was automatically inherited at death by the eldest heir (in most cases male heir). If there was no male heir, the inheritance could be shared among female 'heir-portioners'. The land registers under discussion here relate to heritable property only.

Once the system of notarial recording had become prevalent, attempts were made to introduce a general scheme, and these efforts culminated in the passing of the Registration Act of 1617, which established the Register of Sasines (an 'instrument of sasine' was a document which recorded transfers of ownership; the land itself was said to be 'seised', and the new owner became 'infeft'). Originally a symbolic transfer of earth and stone took place at the time of transfer, sanctioned by a 'precept of sasine' (i.e. mandate from the superior). There were two methods of registration: one was in the General Register (i.e. a national register kept in Edinburgh); the other was in a particular register (i.e. a local register, based on the sheriffdom). These terms to describe registers – general and particular – will crop up again in the discussion of other records. Royal burghs were excluded from this arrangement, and protocol books continued up to 1681 when the burgh registers of sasines were established. To summarize therefore, land outside the burghs was recorded either in the general or particular register; land inside the royal burghs in the burgh register. This situation persisted until 1868, when the particular registers were abolished and all registration transferred to the General Register. This move towards centralization continued with the Burgh Registers (Scotland) Act 1926, which provided for the gradual discontinuation of the burgh registers. This process was completed by the early 1960s, since which time changes in land registration law have led to the phasing out of the traditional sasine transaction. Each property is now recorded on a title sheet to which changes in ownership are added as they occur – a legal development owing much to an administrative practice which originated in the Scottish Record Office in 1875. Search sheets were used to preclude the necessity for successive searches through the registers each time a property was sold. The intention – of saving time – now benefits the local historian who can quickly trace all the deeds relating to any property sold since that time.

Sasine registers are located in the Scottish Record Office. Over two hundred protocol books, mainly from the seventeenth century, are also held (some have been published). These and the burgh registers of sasines are among the records of the individual burghs. The Scottish Record Office has produced an incomplete series of indexes to both the general and particular registers arranged under sheriffdom and covering the seventeenth and early eighteenth centuries. A list can be found in *Sectional List 24* to which we have referred before (page 37). From 1781 there were printed abridgements to sasines, particular and general being included together and arranged according to county. For many purposes these will be sufficient for the amateur historian, and there is the advantage that they may be found in your local history library. The early abridgements were not indexed in the printed text, though the Scottish Record Office has manuscript indexes and you may find that your local history library has indexed its own collections. Those from 1869 included printed indexes under person and place, and appeared annually. For the non-indexed periods, progress can sometimes be made by referring back from references in later sasines.

Sasine records are of value in three areas in particular. First, they can tell the genealogical researcher the names of relatives from whom property was inherited and where they were living (important sometimes for deciding which parish registers to consult). Secondly they are a source of information about topography and land ownership, as the sasine describes the parameters and contents in some detail. Thirdly they are an important source of economic data, in the indications they can give of prosperity in the local community. If, for example, large sections of an estate are being sold or 'mortgaged', one will suspect that the family fortunes are in decline. A possible project in connection with a parish or village would be to look at all the sasines within a specific period, and to construct a profile of the economic situation of the community and its inhabitants.

There were several types of transaction which could be entered in sasine registers, and only a few of the more common can be mentioned here. A key year is 1858. Before that date, the instrument of sasine itself was recorded on behalf of the purchaser, whose name appears at the beginning of the entry. After that date the deed of conveyance (i.e. the sale) was registered in its stead, so it is the seller's name which will appear first. A 'feu charter' or 'feu disposition' recorded a subinfeudation, i.e. the creation of a new feudal estate and a new superior in the chain of superiors and vassals. Incidentally, superiority could be bought and sold independently of land itself. 'Casualties' (i.e. obligations) attached to feudal estates included payment of feu duty to the superior. Charters of 'confirmation' or 'resignation' recorded the superior's acceptance of a new vassal (his title to the lands he had bought or been granted was incomplete without such a charter). Alterations were recorded in a 'charter of novodamus'. A 'disposition', which was the most common form of transaction in recent times, recorded an outright sale of an already established feudal estate. Before the advent of building societies, loans or 'mortgages' were obtained from individuals in most cases. The latter naturally held rights in security over the property as an insurance against non-payment. They laid claim to their rights by recording their bond, the usual form of words used being 'bond and disposition in security'. When the loan was paid off, the debtor recorded his 'discharge'. A mortgagee could still sell the land under burden of a bond, and the bond-holder too could sell or transfer his interest in the property, in a transaction called an 'assignation'.

For the researcher exclusively interested in his own house, earlier sasines may be disappointing. If the house was part of an estate (as would generally be the case in rural areas) it would be mentioned only in the context of transfers of the estate as a whole: whilst for property in burghs there is the problem of identifying houses, because of vagueness in the definition of the location.

The Record of Service of Heirs (from 1847) and its predecessor the Record of Retours, which originated in the fourteenth century, provide an important series of records for the historian up to 1964, when the register virtually ceased. The Record established the right of an heir to enter into his succession: in other words he had to prove his relationship to the deceased. Confirmation of the claim would subsequently be made in the sasine register by recording the service in a notarial instrument (a short cut was to record a precept of *clare constat* from the superior). The service worked as follows: a 'brieve' was issued from the government department known as Chancery, ordering the local sheriff to appoint a jury to ascertain what properties the deceased possessed and the identity of the rightful heir, the verdict of the jury being 'retoured' (i.e. sent back) to Chancery. Incidentally the brieve was the standard method of initiating court actions before 1532, a short writ being despatched from Chancery in the form of a command in the king's name requiring an official (sheriff for example) to prosecute. The Records of Retours are held in the Scottish Record Office, but abridgements for the years 1544–1699 have been published in three volumes, *Inquisitionum ad Capellam Regis Retornatarum Abbreviato*. For the period 1700–1860 there are printed decennial indexes, though there are only a few sets in the country. From 1860 annual indexes were published. These records will be of particular value to the family historian.

In the study of your home, there are records which enable you to flesh out the framework of legal fact with information about the social environment. Prominent among these are the registers of testaments in which may be preserved inventories of the contents of your house at different times. As mentioned above, this moveable property has in Scots law a different history from that of heritable property. Both types were inherited according to fixed laws, but only in the case of moveables could a beneficiary be chosen by the testator. Heritable property was passed down according to primogeniture, whereby the eldest (male) child inherited, subject to a widow's retention of one-third of the estate during her life-time (known as her 'liferent'). In regard to moveable property, the testator could bequeath one-third to whom he pleased (another third went to the widow and the final third to his children). The inheritance of moveable property was originally the responsibility of the commissary courts (see page 49); and even later when the business was transferred to the sheriff court (in 1823) the name 'commissary' was retained for this aspect of its work.

As in the case of the Record of Heirs, the onus was upon the prospective beneficiaries to establish their claim, a process effected through the executor nominated in the will (where a will exists the procedure is known as testament testamentary). Where there is no will (i.e. the deceased is intestate) the procedure is called testament dative. In the latter case a person claiming to act as executor (on the strength of kinship, or in some cases in the capacity of creditor of the deceased) puts forward his reasons for being appointed. The court will confirm this position in its *register of confirmations*, where it will also record the *bonds of caution* submitted (caution is the security provided by the executor to guarantee the proper completion of his task). An inventory of the deceased's property (excluding lands and buildings) is drawn up and lodged with the court by the executor, where it is entered in its register of testaments, together with the names of executors, the date of death and a copy of the will if there is one.

This system can be traced back in general terms to the thirteenth century, but the earliest surviving registers of testaments date only from the sixteenth century (Edinburgh 1514, Dunblane 1539, Glasgow 1547 and St Andrews 1549). All the records of the original commissary courts are now held by the Scottish Record Office, whilst the record of the commissary division of the sheriff courts will be engrossed with their respective court archives. Indexes of all records have been published up to 1800 by the Scottish Record Society, and for the years 1801–23 there are typescript indexes. For part of the nineteenth century there is a printed *Index to Personal Estates of Defuncts* (Edinburgh, including Haddington and Linlithgow 1827–65; other commissariots 1846–67). From 1876 onwards there is an annual printed *Calendar of Confirmations and Inventories granted and given up by the Seven Commissariots of Scotland.* Lists of commissariots and the parishes served by each are given in Gerald Hamilton-Edwards (1983).

It was remarked by J. M. Thomson (1922) that 'though Scottish wills have been so largely drawn upon for family history, little use has been made of them as yet for social history'. He would have been thinking in particular of the scope afforded for analysis of household and personal possessions in terms of their functions and contribution to the overall organization of the domestic economy. A visit to a local museum may give you the chance to see artefacts similar to those described (you may even see them being used in a living reconstruction). You may indeed become interested enough to make a collection of your own, of bygones, family heirlooms and old photographs. The pace of technological change today is such that equipment of relatively recent date – even 20 or 30 years ago – can have considerable historical interest. Published diaries, autobiographies, novels and household accounts can add another dimension to your study: you can find out what sort of food was eaten, how it was prepared and how the evenings were spent. Oral interviews can provide supplementary information; you can at the same time take along examples or photographs of artefacts and ask for a demonstration or description of their use. Advertisements from old newspapers will provide yet another source of information, and your local history library may have early publicity material of gas and electric firms.

The Register of Entails or Tailzies was instituted in 1685. Entail was a process whereby the succession to heritable property could be fixed for generations ahead, the aim being usually to preserve an estate intact, in an effort to maintain the status of an aristocratic family. It became notorious for its crippling effect on agricultural improvement, for it prevented the sale of any part of the property in perpetuity. There were two consequences: able new agriculturalists were unable to buy land (up to one-third of land was burdened in this way); and for families which had fallen on hard times, it proved impossible to mortgage or sell off parts of a property in order to finance the improvement of the remainder. According to Adam Smith, entail was founded 'on the most absurd of all suppositions, the supposition that every successive generation of men have not an equal right to the earth'. The creation of new entails has been prohibited since 1914. Because of the strict conditions governing entailed property, building improvements which could be charged upon the estates were recorded in registers of improvements on entailed estates, which are part of sheriff court archives and cover the period 1770 to the late nineteenth century. The registers contain bills, accounts and estimates. If you are lucky, you may find information about your own property.

The registers we have been considering so far have in common that they relate primarily to legal transactions such as sales or inheritance. Another group of registers has a basically administrative function, in connection with direct taxation, which in respect of local administration at least has nearly always been property-based. One exception is the Poll Tax of 1693–8 levied on individuals, though this was a national tax introduced to pay debts incurred by the armed forces. From the same period comes the Hearth Tax of 1692 which, however, like the Poll Tax, is of most value to the family historian, listing as it does householders rather than properties. The Window Taxes 1747–98 (levied according to the number of windows and leading to a tendency to board them up) and the Inhabited Houses Tax 1778–99, listing servants, carts, carriages, horses and dogs are, like the Poll Tax and Hearth Tax, engrossed within the Exchequer records (E) in the Scottish Record Office.

The land tax was the precursor of our local rating system. In the Middle Ages there was no regularized system of taxation, burghs for example having feu charters by which they paid a lump sum fixed in perpetuity. Negotiations therefore had to be conducted by the Exchequer to extend land taxes (first introduced on a regular basis in 1643 and known popularly as the 'cess') to within the burghs. Even so, the lack of 'diligence' (debt recovery enforcement) made the land tax difficult to collect, a problem which afflicted other taxation initiatives such as the Window Tax. The cess became annual after the Union, and valuation rolls were compiled under the auspices of the commissioners of supply. In the use of these records, however, it must be remembered that the number of landowners was fairly limited, and depending on the method of assessment adopted in any area, once again you may not find specific references to your property, even if it dates from that period. Valuation records remain erratic up to 1854 when the Valuation of Lands Act instituted annual assessment in the counties for services such as roads, prisons and police. Burghal rating practice remained chaotic and varied despite the regularization brought about by the series of burgh police acts through the nineteenth century. A detailed analysis appears in S. H. Turner, *The History of Local Taxation in Scotland*, Blackwood, 1908.

The post-1854 valuation rolls are a major source of information about property, its use, rateable value, and the names and occupations of tenants and proprietors. The compilation of county valuation rolls became a responsibility of county councils in 1889, and these rolls included valuations for police burghs and small royal burghs. From 1929 all burghs were included with the exception of the four counties of cities. In 1974, responsibility was transferred to the regional councils.

Some early rolls have been published, including Poll Tax and Hearth Tax records. Series of rolls since 1854 will possibly be held in your local history library (in some cases on microfiche or microfilm). Full sets are held by the Scottish Record Office (VR). Used imaginatively they can yield a great deal of local information. Size, structure, wealth and distribution of population can be monitored; changing economic activity can be studied through an analysis of occupations (the rolls can be effectively used in this regard alongside the census enumeration books); and the development of a village and town can be traced by recording new streets as they appear.

Using registers efficiently

An analytical approach to the use of registers is of vital importance, and now that we have surveyed several of those which relate to property, we can consider one or two general principles that will contribute to a more efficient exploitation. Many historical records are lists of one kind or another – registers, rentals and accounts – and when faced with this material, there is not much point in wading through in a desultory manner copying down extracts at random. The researcher must be looking for the answer to specific questions. To take an example from our current quest – the history of a house – one avenue we could pursue is to investigate changing patterns of ownership. Once we have formulated an idea such as this, we must next know how to set about a systematic study, for which a standard procedure is to propose an hypothesis, on the analogy of methods developed in the natural sciences, the hypothesis being established *before* the data are collected and *before* the experiment is carried out. You will not, after all, be in a position to make a discovery if you do not know what it is you are trying to prove or disprove.

One hypothesis we could make is as follows: the trend for professional people to acquire rural cottages as second homes began before the second world war. Now, assuming that we have the information available to answer this hypothesis in the affirmative or negative, we can see that the proof presented, and not any accumulation of facts, is our contribution, original contribution, to historical thought; and when it is understood that such a procedure is what constitutes research, the idea of it immediately appears much more exciting. For you have a definite goal: each piece of information is being collected for a specific purpose, to test your hypothesis, everything else being ruthlessly ignored, because it is irrelevant to your needs. You do not get bogged down with facts, which can become tedious and meaningless if not moulded into life by your intelligence and curiosity. Consider too that you will make a contribution of value to others, even professional historians. They have no time for an indigestible soup of facts – they are much too busy; but your thesis, if soundly argued, can be quickly assimilated and possibly incorporated as an element in a more general study.

The hypothesis used as an example here can be tested most effectively by means of statistical techniques, which are now used a great deal in historical research. You are advised to have a look at one of the many introductory textbooks on the subject, and to follow up further ideas in monographs written specifically from the viewpoint of historical research. The essential point about statistical studies is that you need take only a sample of the available data, which in current census interpretation, for example, comprises ten per cent of the population under consideration. This is regarded as sufficient for providing reliable generalizations, though there is one proviso – it must be what is known as a random sample, a concept which is explained in detail in textbooks of statistics.

One other aspect of this subject needs to be mentioned – the problem of formulating good hypotheses. It is the most skilful part of the work, and the one to which a good deal of attention should be paid, long before you become deeply involved in your material. The best source is the current consensus or debate on a subject, against which the local situation can be matched. A good hypothesis also needs to have certain qualities, some of which can be briefly outlined here. First, it must not be so trivial as to be self-evident (in recent years there has been some lapse on the part of professional historians in this respect). A hypothesis such as 'there was a growth of trade in Scotland in the eighteenth century' is neither original nor stimulating. Yet in some cases of current research, so much attention has been paid to the desirability of using primary sources, as if this was a virtue in itself, that the historian has not spent any time thinking of interesting questions to ask of this material. The finished work is dull because the hypothesis being tested is dull as well. On the other hand, hypotheses must not be too large; they must be tailored to the available information. Take the example we used: if there were no valuation rolls, we would find difficulty in carrying out our projected study. So it would be pointless to make the hypothesis: it would be valuable only in metaphysics. Hypotheses must not be too large for the material; but equally they must not be too large for you. How much searching will it take to test your theory, and how much time do you have to spare? A final and most important quality is that you must suspect that your hypothesis is true, or at least that there will be a significant result one way or the other. To take it to ridiculous lengths, a proposition that most houses used to be painted red is not only going to be proved false, but also the fact of its being false tells us nothing either; whereas our hypothesis about rural home ownership, even if answered in the negative, still represents an interesting discovery. In the latter case, we would probably want to go on to find out when the trend *did* start, so in that respect it can be preferable to predict accurately in the first place, even though the information about the earlier period is not wasted if it helps to confirm the revised hypothesis. Accurate formulation of theories is of course an art which cannot be learned in a rule book. What must be avoided however (despite the strong temptation that might exist) is doctoring the facts to make them conform if your thesis has proved to be unsubstantiated.

Considerations such as those outlined above should contribute to an efficient use of the many registers relating to property which have been discussed. To conclude this section, we turn to a miscellaneous group of historical materials that can also be exploited for research into housing. One vitally important source not considered so far is maps and plans, particularly the large-scale Ordnance Survey maps published since the middle of the nineteenth century. Maps are valuable in two respects at least: first, they can tell you the age of your house; and secondly they record any alterations or extensions to its exterior. Interestingly, maps will only show horizontal extensions, not vertical ones. For the vertical face you can turn to another major primary source – photographs – which, like maps, can be found in your local history library as well as in the major national collection, the National Monuments Record (arranged topographically by town or parish). If your house is older than the nineteenth century, it may be featured in one of the detailed estate maps from the eighteenth century. Town plans in the main date only from the early nineteenth century and often include names of proprietors or tenants of individual houses. Another major nineteenth-century category is feuing plans engrossed in estate and sheriff court records; these bear witness to the rising power of entrepreneurial and professional classes who built themselves grand villas on the outskirts of burghs, thereby creating in some places the first major suburbs.

The social connotations of house building styles have been studied by urban geographers and they have identified a recurring pattern whereby influences percolate downwards through the class structure. For example, the once fashionable Regency terraces on the perimeters of town centres can be seen as the model for middle-class suburban rows and at the bottom of the social scale for terraces of farm cottages. As each style was popularized, the social elite introduced another: the late nineteenth-century town mansions discussed above aped the country houses of the landed gentry with their surrounding parks, and in turn were copied by lower middle-class bungalows (with additional colonial influences) in the 1930s, the cycle being completed by today's housing estates with their postage-stamp gardens.

You could make a study of houses and their owners in your area to assess the accuracy of this model. A related aspect is the degeneration of property at the centre of towns as the affluent move outwards: in each successive generation, an area becomes dominated by a lower social class, though in recent years the process may have turned full circle, as inner cities have again become fashionable – but possibly for different types of people from the original inhabitants who inspired their construction. To study the process, valuation rolls can be used, to monitor both the relative valuations of property over time and the social status of the occupiers.

Housing conditions can make an interesting study. Few properties in Scotland predate the eighteenth century – building with stone is a relatively recent phenomenon, especially in rural areas. Conditions of rural cottages from the early period can be studied in estate archives – when new leases were granted, for example, surveys of the properties were sometimes made. In the burghs, there are some sixteenth- and even fifteenth-century houses, already featuring the typically Scottish tenement construction that came to be such an important element of nineteenth-century industrial cities. These latter tenements consisted of one- and two-roomed flats with minimal sanitary facilities – a communal sink on each landing and a single privy at ground level. The appalling conditions in which people lived led to the introduction of a much stricter system of control, and the records generated as a result can be used in a study of housing conditions from that time forward. In the burghs, housing and environment were the responsibility of the dean of guild, whose minute books and archives of approved duplicate plans can be consulted. Depending on the size of the burgh concerned, the county council planning records may also be relevant; in the case of small burghs, building warrants and planning applications were handled separately by town councils and county councils respectively. In rural areas, county councils dealt with both aspects of construction work control. Current responsibility lies with the district councils. Details of many buildings can also be found in the archives of fire insurance companies. For more general information about housing conditions, you could use the annual reports of medical officers of health and sanitation officers, both of which officials were very conscious of the importance of good-quality housing stock. The same is true of the registrar general (responsible for censuses), whose published annual reports are based upon census and registration data. The government too was concerned about nineteenth-century housing and important commissions were set up, notably the Poor Law Commission into the Sanitary Conditions of the Working Population (reported 1842) and the Royal Commission on the Housing of the Industrial Population of Scotland (1917), which led to the first major council-house building programmes.

Historic buildings

A natural extension to the study of private houses is the consideration of other buildings in your locality – private castles and mansions, and public buildings such as tollbooths, churches and government offices. Some of these have been looked at already in specific contexts – schools, churches and prisons for example – but in all cases the records we have been looking at so far in this chapter will also have general relevance, as will some of the questions that were asked: what materials they were built from, what style of architecture was employed, what were and are their functions and how did these affect the shape and location of the buildings. In looking at public buildings, concentration on this latter aspect gives scope for an interesting project analysing the different roles which buildings perform. Fundamentally of course they provide shelter, but the growing sophistication of a civilization can be gauged by an increasing complexity of function. One archaeological model in fact tries to measure stages in growth both by the relative *number* of structures in a settlement and the number of *attributes* (i.e. uses) that can be differentiated. After shelter, for instance, perhaps the most common early use of a building was for defence. The military historian might be interested in the study of locational factors and styles of fortification which were a response to military technologies available. Progressively, as lawlessness came to be controlled, defensive considerations became less important, the interesting consequence being that the land magnate was afforded greater freedom to use buildings as a vehicle for expressing dominant aesthetic values (Georgian mansions for example are said to proclaim ideals of harmony and stability dear to the eighteenth-century aristocracy).

A possible project is to monitor local styles of architecture and to attempt the difficult task of relating them to social and economic factors. The promotion of an image can be studied in other types of building as well. For example, a seventeenth-century townhouse could be compared with its counterpart from the nineteenth century to bring out the different values projected by the builders. Whereas the one will probably be an example of the Scottish domestic style, the other will likely follow Roman models. Why is this and what impression were the builders trying to give?

Architectural style is only one facet of the growing diversification of buildings. Another possible theme is to explore the uses of them in terms of growing specialization. Early courts for example were hardly separated from the baron's castle – they would be held in the hall or an open meeting place alongside. But growing sophistication led to the appearance of court buildings, as well as meeting places for town councils to be a focus and symbol of their authority; prisons (which again would originally have been in the baron's castle); and later still industrial and commercial premises. You could trace the rise of any of these types; or, if you are more interested in recent times, you could look at the origin of shops in your town. At what time and for what reasons did they supplant the traditional retail outlets – markets and fairs? A useful source in this study is the Shop

Tax Assessments 1785–9(E).

Local history libraries usually have good collections of material about historic buildings, and you should start your investigations there. If you live in one of the areas for which the Royal Commission on the Ancient and Historical Monuments of Scotland has produced an inventory, use it to establish the basic background information. Another unfinished series as far as Scotland is concerned is the Pevsner one on the architecture of different regions, published by Penguin; only two volumes had been produced by the end of 1984. Parish and county historians will often have a lot to say about historic buildings, and there will of course be guide books to specific houses, which your library will have. Two monumental works from the nineteenth century are R. W. Billings, *The Baronial and Ecclesiastical Antiquities of Scotland*, Blackwood, 1845–52, and D. MacGibbon and T. Ross, *Castellated and Domestic Architecture of Scotland*, David Douglas, 1887–92 (reprinted Mercat Press, 1971). Your local history library is also likely to have series of photographs of famous buildings and topographical prints from the pre-photographic age. These more often than not depict the castle, mansion or historic church. Remember too that the original text that accompanied the prints will concentrate on topographical description – indeed in the eighteenth century landowners paid to have their seats included. The architectural section of the National Monuments Record has a huge collection of photographs – about a quarter of a million – and an equal number of plans, reports and estate papers. The Ordnance Survey topographical sheets already mentioned in connection with prehistoric sites are also relevant. Among tools for the researcher at the National Monuments Record are a card catalogue arranged alphabetically by place, and a survey guide arranged by county giving details of records held elsewhere – in the Scottish Record Office, the National Library of Scotland and private collections. Accessions are listed in the annual *Discovery and Excavation in Scotland*. The Historic Buildings Division of the Scottish Development Department, 25 Drumsheugh Gardens, Edinburgh EH3 7RN (telephone 031 226 3611) serves the same functions in respect of historic buildings as the Ancient Monuments Division for prehistoric sites.

For the oldest buildings, from the medieval period, few records remain, and the buildings themselves have not fared much better; most of course were not made of stone or brick. The best-preserved records are those relating to crown properties, of which information on structure and contents is to be found in the *Exchequer Rolls*, supplemented and later superseded by the *Accounts of the Lord High Treasurer* 1473–1635 and the *Accounts of the Masters of Work* 1529–1679, all of which are published. The history of crown buildings can also be studied in Robert Scott Mylne, *The Master Masons to the Crown of Scotland and their Works*, Scott & Fergusson: Burgess & Co.,

1893. For the period after the Union, the records of the King's Remembrancer's Office 1708–1837 and its successor the King's and Lord Treasurer's Remembrancer's Office 1837–1930 (among Exchequer records in the Scottish Record Office) contains information about a wide variety of crown buildings, both civil and military. The latter are also featured in the eighteenth-century Board of Ordnance maps, some of which are held in the National Library of Scotland Map Room (others are in London's Public Record Office). For the modern period, the records of commissioners of crown estates 1830–50 are followed by those of the Ministry of Public Buildings and Works, now the Department of the Environment, whose Scottish records are deposited with the Scottish Record Office. The Department also has a library, the Property Services Agency Library, Argyle House, Edinburgh EH3 9SJ. It boasts a collection of around 250,000 photographs of both government buildings and ancient monuments, together with a large number of plans.

For historic monuments not under government control, there is nothing like this detailed wealth or continuity of evidence. Buildings belonging to burghs can be investigated through town council minutes and the miscellaneous plans and documents often listed as the final sections in burgh inventories prepared by archivists. For private buildings the main primary sources are family and estate papers and, in the case of those affected, the forfeited estate records. If you are interested in early keeps and castles – and what area of Scotland is not littered with them, in varying stages of collapse, exciting our curiosity every time we take a walk or drive in the countryside? – try first to establish which families built them and inhabited them. You should in most cases be able to get this information from the various published sources mentioned above, but failing that, the methods outlined in the next chapter for determining the boundaries of baronies and estates will be applicable. Once the ownership pattern is known, the relevant family papers, either published or unpublished, can be consulted, having their whereabouts established through the National Register of Archives.

The techniques outlined in this chapter should enable you to make a general survey of the buildings in your area, establishing their approximate dates and the functions they performed in the local community. A stage further in this process would be to consider them in their relationships with one another and in the general context of the development of the settlement of which they form a part, a subject which is the theme of the next chapter.

Chapter Six

SETTLEMENT STUDIES: HISTORY OF A VILLAGE, TOWN OR PARISH

The history of one's village, town or parish is the most obvious subject that comes to mind in response to the question 'what is local history and what sort of projects can one become involved in?'. Such is often the theme adopted by local history groups. However, it will be evident from what has been discussed so far that there are many other options open, and indeed, that this particular theme is one that needs to be handled with care. Attention has already been drawn to the random collection of data from different periods of a community's history that passes as parish history in some antiquarian books, and in order to avoid such diffuseness it is necessary to establish a unifying and consistent frame of reference. One unifying thread may seem obvious – the landscape of the parish itself – but it does not follow that anything that has ever happened there is fit for inclusion, merely on the strength of that connection.

A typical Scottish parish may have been inhabited in prehistoric times – evident in the remains of hill forts, standing stones and enclosures in now uninhabited moorland. From medieval times we may find a keep on a rise or hill, now often isolated and ruinous. From the eighteenth century there may survive a clustered settlement of low stone houses – perhaps hand-loom weavers' cottages – around the parish church; whilst the nineteenth century may have bequeathed an industrial mill complex along the river.

Already, arising from this schematic outline, there are a host of questions that can be asked. Why did prehistoric peoples choose such inhospitable sites? Perhaps they were pastoralists and the lowland at that time was a bog. Why was the protection of the castle not needed in the seventeenth century? The development of artillery had made it redundant, and (possibly as a result) the period of blood-feuding was over. Why was the river not utilized earlier for generating power? The complex technology, markets or mercantile capital were not available. Equally one can look at a locality and ask 'why did something *not* happen here?'. There is perhaps a fast-flowing river, but industry did not develop. To answer, we might look at the settlement's location – the roads and rail system, for instance. Was the region economically isolated?

The internal structure and layout of settlements can also be a fascinating study. Why are some streets straight whilst others follow a winding path? Is physical geography the determining factor, or are there other causes?

These questions have in common a concentration on the structure, functions and locations of settlements in the context of man's interaction with his environment. Other types of material sometimes included in parish histories – church records, famous national events that occurred in the locality, notes on poor relief, and famous sons and daughters – refer in the main to quite different issues and it makes for a more effective and unified project if they are excluded. If you wish to pursue social, political and human history in a local context, all well and good, but these themes should be pursued separately and should only be included in the study of a settlement in so far as they have affected the physical or human geography of the area. A parish church, for example, can be considered from the point of view of its location within the settlement: in a burgh it will often be outside the old town walls as burials were sometimes not permitted inside and sufficient land was often not available for grandiose buildings. Such a phenomenon may incidentally make us rethink our ideas about the functions of town walls (high burgh tenements may have been the main defence). It will also be valid in this context to investigate the economic prosperity that paid for the church's construction, but not the famous preachers that preached there or the history of the incumbent ministers.

One advantage in approaching the subject of parish history in this way is that one can exploit the findings of archaeologists and geographers, which can in some small measure compensate for the paucity of early written records. Archaeology can tell us about former configurations of a settlement, about its culture and economy, and, as we have seen, about earlier settlements which may have completely disappeared and whose existence may not even have been otherwise suspected. Geography can tell us how the exigencies of soil, climate and terrain have influenced settlement patterns and how human activity has modified and exploited this environment. The cross-fertilization of geography and history in settlement studies has produced a hybrid discipline known as *historical geography*, and the remainder of this chapter will pursue themes within this context: the *parameters of settlement* (physical geography and climate); the *structure and interrelationships of settlements* (through a study of topographical maps and communication systems); and finally *human geography* (in the activities of man in farming, trade and industry).

Models

The interrelationships of the factors outlined above in the context of a settlement have been schematized by models developed in analytical archaeology. Models are methodological tools widely used in many disciplines, but the most effective are often those with spatial applications (it is easier to make a diagram of geometric space, which has physical properties, than it is, say, of time, which is intangible). Settlement studies, therefore, are ideal for their application: by taking a frozen moment from the past and reconstructing as far as one is able the entire environment, one can then assess the interaction of forces, natural and man-made, that have brought a settlement to that particular stage in its development.

Models can best be understood through an analogy – that of a person who has never seen a car confronted for the first time with an engine. He is in the position of an historian confronted by historical records. How do all the bits relate to one another? What is the purpose of the whole system? He is not likely to make much progress by random tinkering; he needs to understand something of the underlying principles, the structure and purpose of the engine. A model can be seen as a set of general principles or a schematic simplification; and once it has been understood, it becomes much easier both to grasp the system as a whole, and to ask specific relevant questions about any part of it. The historian is not claiming that history is like an internal combustion engine. What he is saying is that historical forces can only be understood by the impact they have (this is how a scientist studies sub-atomic particles which similarly have theoretical existence only); and just as a physicist measures mechanical forces with scales and meters of one kind and another, so the historian can use models to measure historical forces.

The line between a model and a hypothesis is not clear-cut; but a model tends to be a whole system of interacting parts whilst an hypothesis is a particular question to which one is seeking an answer. Use of a model enables one to formulate better hypotheses. It is not, therefore, something which one is trying to prove true or false; rather it is a complete entity which may or may not be applicable to a particular situation.

Some models are very broad in scope, underpinning the very processes of thought. Modern historical research for example is to some extent founded on a behaviourist model, in which man's responses are judged to be determined by external social factors. Contrast this outlook with that of earlier historians, who tended to emphasize man's individuality and freedom of action. This is not to say that we are right and earlier historians were wrong. Part of the excitement of studying history is that it is an intellectual game which all can play, and the results are different (though equally interesting) depending upon the rules adopted.

Other models are used to analyse quite specific processes – by means of systems analysis for example. One noticeable recent development, in fact, is the way such models, devised in one discipline, have been applied to quite different areas. In history, for example, the concept of optimal survival strategies owes much to cybernetics; and economic historians will make use of economic models such as Rostow's of an economy's take-off into self-sustained growth when the growth rate exceeds two per cent per annum.

To construct a model involves the schematization and simplification of reality, and in this process lie two inherent dangers. The first is that the researcher expends most of his energy refining and complicating his model to make it applicable in detail to a given situation. In the process, however, it becomes more and more abstruse and the historian's obsession with its application begins to replace his interest in his subject. The second danger lies in the opposite direction: of simplying reality to fit the model. The better middle course is to see models principally as a device for formulating pertinent hypotheses, in which the researcher does not succumb to a rigid servitude. Used in this way, they can suggest many avenues of research.

Physical geography

The physical geography of an area dictates the environment with which man contends in his struggle, initially for survival, subsequently for prosperity. Three basic aspects are considered here – soil, geology and climate.

The first major land utilization survey of Great Britain took place between the wars under the leadership of L. Dudley Stamp. The results appeared in *The Land of Britain: the Report of the Land Utilization Survey of Britain*, published in regional parts between 1937 and 1946. The part for your area should be available in your local history library. More recently the Macaulay Institute for Soil Research in Aberdeen has produced two sets of maps for Scotland (seven in each set, at scale 1:250,000) – one illustrating land capability and the other soil types. An interpretative handbook accompanies the maps. In addition the Macaulay Institute has conducted in-depth surveys in some areas which have resulted in larger scale 1:25,000 maps and more detailed monographs. All their publications are listed in their annual *Publications List*.

Geological mapping is the responsibility of the British Geological Survey (formerly the Institute of Geological Science), Murchison House, West Mains Road, Edinburgh EH9 3LA. There are three main series: an older set of 1:253,440 (for solid geology), which is being replaced by one at 1:250,000; an older series of 1:63,360 (separate maps for solid and drift geology) which is being replaced by one at 1:50,000; and the largest scale, 1:10,560, still incomplete and consisting of some printed and some dyeline editions. Geological memoirs (detailed analytical accounts of defined localities) have been produced by the Survey since the beginning of the century and can be complemented by the series of six volumes of regional geologies covering the whole of Scotland (these are revised periodically). More specialist material from the British Geological Survey includes coalfield papers (the development of Scottish mining can be linked to the exploitation of progressively deeper seams), memoirs of economic geology, mineral assessment reports, memoirs of palaeontology (i.e. fossils) and geochemical atlases. A full list of current publications appears in *Sectional List No. 45* of HMSO Government publications (updated periodically). Information about the British Geological Survey can be found in R. B. Wilson, *A History of the Geological Survey in Scotland*, Natural Environment Research Council: Institute of Geological Sciences, 1977. For those who would like a less technical approach to geology, the excursion guides of local geological associations are recommended.

Maps of annual rainfall are published by the Meteorological Office, 231 Corstorphine Road, Edinburgh EH12 7BB. The same body also produces information packs on the past history of severe weather conditions; climatological summaries for a number of locations; a general synopsis, *Scotland's Climate: Some Facts and Figures*, and a series of 13 booklets on the climate of different regions of Scotland. Much of this material is specifically prepared for use in school and college projects.

Topographical maps and plans

Environmental factors provide a framework in which to study man's activities in the landscape; and central to the latter investigation are topographical maps and plans which have recorded the resulting human settlement patterns.

The earliest surviving maps of Scotland date from the second half of the sixteenth century, in atlases produced by Dutch cartographers and engravers such as Mercator and Blaeu. The first regional maps were a series of six in John Speed's *Kingdome of Scotland* of 1610, and county maps (46 in all) first appeared in Blaeu's Atlas of 1654. These maps were based upon others drawn at the beginning of the century by Timothy Pont (the manuscript versions of which are held by the National Library of Scotland) and revised by Robert Gordon of Straloch in the 1630s and 1640s.

A Scottish cartographer, John Adair, arguing that a revision of Blaeu's maps was very necessary, was given authority by the Privy Council around 1680 to 'take a survey of the whole shires of the kingdom, and to make up mapps thereof, describing each shire, royal burgh and other towns considerable, the houses of the nobility and gentry, the most considerable rivers, lochs . . . etc.'. Adair seems to have encountered difficulties in publication: in 1703 *The Description of the Sea Coast and Islands of Scotland* appeared, but many of his other maps, of which he left 28 on his death in 1718, remained in manuscript form. They may have been used by Herman Moll in his *Set of 36 New and Correct Maps of Scotland Divided into Shires*, 1725, a set which was followed by a new collection by Thomas Kitchen in

1749 in an atlas entitled *Geographiae Scotiae*.

The *Military Survey of Scotland* 1747–55 was an urgent response to the Jacobite rebellion of 1745, the work being carried out principally by William Roy. The original intention was to map the Highlands only, but southern Scotland was afterwards added. The maps are held by the British Library in London, but your local history library should have photocopies or photographic prints.

The second half of the eighteenth century saw a proliferation of county maps, including series by Andrew and Mostyn Armstrong, John Ainslie and Matthew Stobie. Complete atlases of Scotland were produced by Thomas Brown in 1807 (25 county maps), John Lothian in 1827 (33 county maps) and by John Thomson, who published the first large-scale maps of counties, some of which were new surveys whilst others drew on older work.

Meanwhile, during the eighteenth century these and other cartographers had been active in the production of estate maps, which give a minutely detailed picture of the Scottish countryside (and quite often burghs as well, where they happen to fall within the areas of large estates). The background to this activity was the agricultural improvement movement, which began as early as the seventeenth century with pioneers such as Cockburn of Ormiston, but for which the main impetus came in the second half of the eighteenth century. In the Highlands, the process was still at work well into the nineteenth century.

The improvers were intent upon a radical reorganization of farming methods. Traditionally, an estate was not divided up into fields as we understand them; instead there was a section devoted exclusively to arable, divided into an 'infield' which was cultivated in thin strips called 'rigs', separated by 'baulks' where all the weeds and rubbish were sometimes dumped, and an 'outfield' – poorer land alternately sown with oats and left fallow. Beyond the outfield the tenants and cottars grazed their animals together on the 'commons' or 'commonties'. The landowners wanted to do two things: first to abolish the rig system and to replace it with larger field units; and second to enclose the commons and divide up the land amongst themselves (enclosure did not in the main cause the social and economic disruption that was the case in England, as under Scots law tenants did not usually have any traditional rights in common land).

Both enclosure and division of runrig (i.e. where rigs of different ownership were mixed together) could take place by agreement among the landowners concerned, and this method was employed frequently in the seventeenth century and after. However, two major acts of 1695 gave legal sanction and encouragement to the practice. First, the Commonty Act gave general supervisory powers to the Court of Session with, in most cases, the actual details of the division being handled by sheriffs, justices of the peace or lords of regality. This differed from the English practice, where a local act of

Parliament was required.

The 1695 Runrig Act similarly gave powers of implementation to sheriffs and justices of the peace, but also included an extra clause which allowed a division to be forced by any one of the parties involved regardless of the wishes of the remainder. In probably the majority of cases there was no problem, because the landowner owned all the rigs on a particular estate, and all that was required was that he draw up in conjunction with his surveyor a map of all the individual rigs and their tenants (the usual practice was for them to be allocated a variety of unconnected rigs so that all shared alike in the good and poor land) and apportion to them new farms roughly equivalent to their original holdings. The map will show the names of the rig holders and crops being grown. In these cases no legal action was required.

The situation differed either where there were major landowners who held rigs that were inextricably tangled together, or (in a few cases) where small landowners or 'feuars' (see page 124) owned one or two rigs. In these cases, recourse was necessary to the sheriff courts, and, in extreme cases, to the Court of Session itself.

The transformation of the landscape brought about by the twin developments of enclosure and division of runrig was quite profound. In the words of I. Whyte (1979):

> There was a wide conceptual gulf between a holding which consisted of a series of scattered strips among the infields and outfields of a ferme toun and one which was composed of a number of separate, compact and contiguous enclosed fields. The former, by its very nature, involved communal working in many of the operations of farming. The latter was essentially a discrete and self-sufficient unit in terms of labour and equipment, under the direction of one man.

Subsequent to enclosure, the landowners often continued to map their estates at regular intervals for administrative and planning purposes, and such plans often include tabulations of rental and produce – in many cases they are still likely to be the largest-scale maps produced for rural localities.

Burghs, too, had their common lands, which were also enclosed (often to the benefit of the ruling cliques who by this time dominated burgh affairs), and in some cases the earliest town map will result from the transaction. Town plans were made for other purposes, however, the earliest surviving – of Edinburgh in 1544 and Berwick in 1573 – both being drawn in connection with military operations. From the middle of the seventeenth century there have survived plans of Cupar, St Andrews, Edinburgh and Aberdeen surveyed by James Gordon, and major towns were further surveyed in the eighteenth century. The first substantial collection of town maps did not appear until 1828, however, with the production of the *Town*

Atlas of Scotland from surveys by James Wood. It included 48 towns, but Wood also surveyed others which were published independently. In many cases, proprietors of individual houses are shown.

The beginning of the nineteenth century also saw the start of the movement for electoral reform, both in local government and in parliament. For the purposes of the latter, a parliamentary report of 1832, *the Report Upon the Boundaries of the Several Cities, Burghs and Towns in Scotland in Respect of the Election of Members to Serve in Parliament* included plans of the towns concerned, numbering 75 in all.

The most recent addition to our knowledge of the topography of burghs has come from a series of archaeological surveys being carried out by the Department of Archaeology, University of Glasgow. The published volumes for different towns, by Anne Simpson Turner and Sylvia Stevenson, contain reconstructions of early burgh layout, supplemented by written material.

Perhaps the most significant date in Scottish cartography is 1841, when the Ordnance Survey Act was passed. The Ordnance Survey had been in operation before this date, and is generally regarded as having been formally founded in 1791, though its roots are even earlier still, in projects such as the military survey of William Roy mentioned above. But it was only after 1841 that a programme of continuous and systematic mapping of the country was begun. The initial decision was to make the standard survey on the 1:10,560 scale (six inches to a mile), and in the early 1850s six counties were published accordingly: Edinburgh, Fife, Haddington, Kinross, Kirkcudbright and Wigtown, plus the Isle of Lewis. For towns a larger 1:1056 (five feet to a mile) scale was envisaged and surveys undertaken, but at a still early stage it was decided to reorganize the programme as follows: cultivated areas were to be surveyed at 1:2500 (25 inches to the mile), uncultivated areas at 1:10,560 and urban areas with a population in excess of 4,000 at 1:500 (ten feet to the mile). For most areas of the country 1:2500 scale maps have remained the standard survey, whilst uncultivated parts of the Highlands have never been mapped beyond 1:10,560.

The basic 1:2500 maps for cultivated areas were surveyed between 1845 and 1887 and published between 1856 and 1896; a second edition (the first revision) was completed before the First World War. The third edition (second revision) was disrupted by the war and in 1918 it was decided that the revision should take place on a forty-year cycle for all areas with a population density of less than 100 per square mile (previously a twenty-year revision had been envisaged). The latest series of 1:2500 maps was begun in 1948 and completed in the early 1980s.

As mentioned, the larger-scale maps for urban areas began with the 1:1056 scale series of the 1850s which was abandoned in favour of a 1:500 series. This programme began in 1858 but was discontinued in 1894 when it was decided that revision would be carried out only at local cost (some revisions were made under these conditions). Finally, after a period when town plans were produced by enlarging the 1:2500 maps to 1:1250 (50 inches to the mile), a new series of urban surveys on the 1:1250 scale was started in 1943.

The 1:10,560 series began with the six counties mentioned above surveyed in the 1850s. Several revisions have been made, the information in most cases being derived from the 1:2500 series. Other series, such as the 1:63,360 (one inch to a mile) are likewise derived from the larger-scale maps. The three basic series – the 1:1250 for urban areas, the 1:2500 for cultivated areas and the 1:10,560 for uncultivated areas – have continued to the present, the only major change being the introduction of metrication, which has slightly altered the scales used (six-inch maps for example are now 1:10,000 rather than 1:10,560).

The work of the archaeological section of the Ordnance Survey has already been mentioned in connection with the representation of archaeological sites on the general maps. Thematic maps were also produced of, for instance, Roman Britain, Dark Age Britain, Ancient Britain and Monastic Britain.

Details of published Ordnance Survey maps from the earliest surveys to the present are given in J. B. Harley, *Ordnance Survey Maps: a Descriptive Manual*, Ordnance Survey, 1975 and in J. B. Harley and C. W. Phillips, *Historian's Guide to Ordnance Survey Maps*, Standing Conference for Local History: National Council of Social Service, 1964. An indispensable handbook to the early maps of Scotland, including their locations is D. G. Moir, *The Early Maps of Scotland to 1850*, Royal Scottish Geographical Society, Volume 1, 1973, Volume 2, 1983.

You should find that maps relating to your locality are of relatively easy access. Your local history library will probably hold copies of the early county maps of the eighteenth century and before and may well also have photocopies or photographic copies of some, if not all, of the relevant estate plans. It will probably also hold some of the Ordnance Survey series, and if not your District Council Planning Department will definitely have them (there are often facilities available for students). Failing this, there are three major institutions with extensive map collections – the National Library of Scotland, the Scottish Record Office and the National Monuments Record.

The National Library of Scotland Map Room is situated in Causewayside, Edinburgh EH9 1PH, on the site currently being developed as the new Science Reference Library. It contains collections of maps from the middle of the sixteenth century, including the early manuscript maps of Timothy Pont and Robert Gordon. County maps from the eighteenth century are well represented, but the great strength of the collection from the local historian's point of view is its comprehensive holdings of all Ordnance Survey series from the earliest surveys to the present day.

The main features of the collection in the Scottish Record Office are estate maps supplemented by sheriff court plans from the nineteenth century onwards. The collection is housed in West Register House. Plans for the division of common lands submitted to the courts during processes of enclosure form the original core of the estate maps, together with others extracted from family papers in the GD (Gifts and Deposits) inventories. Plans relating to transport and public utilities (including railways and railway buildings, bridges, canals, harbours, tramways, roads, water supply and sewage) originate from sheriff court archives, where they were deposited in connection with developments needing statutory approval. Maps and plans are included in the one inventory (RHP) and the main access is through a card index under place. There are also subject indexes grouping together categories such as architecture, harbours and railways. The Scottish Record Office has produced a free leaflet about its maps and plans, and a complete inventory of its holdings is in process of publication, of which three volumes, compiled by Ian H. Adams, have appeared under the title *Descriptive List of Plans in the Scottish Record Office*, HMSO, Volume 1, 1966, Volume 2, 1970, Volume 3, 1974. A fourth volume is in preparation.

The map collection of the National Monuments Record consists mainly of estate plans deposited or copied in connection with recording buildings on the sites. The collection is integrated with pictorial and architectural material in a topographical arrangement by county.

Map interpretation

Using historical maps is a skilled activity, and it must be emphasized that map evidence can rarely be used alone as a basis for reaching conclusions. Shortcomings include inaccuracies (especially true of pre-Ordnance Survey maps), omission (for example, many early maps do not show roads – which is not to say that roads did not exist) and misleading dating – it must be remembered that the date of publication is not always the date of the survey (there can be discrepancies of up to 50 years between the two). Two more profound limitations belong to possible uses of map evidence: one is that maps show a pattern of buildings, not of settlement (i.e. inhabited buildings); and secondly, in the main they do not show the use of buildings or the historical relationship among them. Juxtaposition of two features does not entail any economic or historical relationship, and the complex factors underlying the growth and location of settlements depend partly on human forces which cannot possibly be represented directly on a map. In some cases human activity can be deduced, from buildings whose functions are clear from their structure or indicated on the map itself, and some maps – estate plans are a good example – go beyond topographical representation to indicate the economic system in operation; but these exceptions apart, maps indicate little about the activity taking place in the landscape. The historian does well to look upon maps as a source of questions rather than answers.

A possible project would be to try to re-create settlement maps for your locality, especially if there are no estate plans available for the period in which you are interested. You could start by buying a large-scale Ordnance Survey map and making copies from it (hand-drawn, not photocopies – photocopying Ordnance Survey maps is illegal) and could tentatively mark in outlines from data obtained about individual buildings discussed in the last chapter and from estate rentals with supplementary maps and archaeological information. An excellent example of what can be achieved by this method is John H. Simpson, 'The Origins of Gifford', *Transactions of the East Lothian Antiquarian and Field Naturalists Society*, Volume XVIII, 1984, pp 5–21. A linked project would be to compile a local trail booklet following the track of forgotten buildings, roads and settlements.

A recent alternative to map evidence has been provided by aerial photography, whose use in connection with archaeology has already been noted. Aerial photographs have the advantage over maps of showing elevations (though not too distinctly in the case of vertical shots – there is an added problem of distortion too). They are also superior to maps in indicating economic activity (the crops being grown for example), in graphically illustrating the physical features of a settlement and in showing a much wider variety of attributes (colour, building materials and so on). A map, like a model, is a schematic simplification; a photograph is more akin to a pair of eyes. The strengths and weaknesses of each stem from this distinction.

As mentioned in the last chapter, aerial photography has benefited archaeological studies in a different area altogether – the recording of crop marks – to such an extent that, in the words of J. K. St. Joseph (1977), 'the speed of discovery is transformed, since air reconnaissance in competent hands can yield discoveries at a rate previously undreamed of'. For example the layout of a medieval village whose traces are now hidden under fields can be accurately plotted, and if such a settlement – or even an unknown and oddly placed building – is to be found in your local landscape, you can investigate the reason for its location and for its demise.

Systematic aerial surveys have formed part of the work of the Royal Commission on the Ancient and Historical Monument of Scotland, principally for archaeological purposes, and the photographs are kept in the archaeological section of the National Monuments Record. Modern landscapes have been regularly photographed by commercial firms since the 1930s, and your local history library should have some examples.

As well as showing the general topographical features of a region, maps and aerial photographs can also be used in an analysis of the internal structure of settlements and the relationships among them, from which it is possible to formulate hypotheses about their origin and growth.

Rural settlements tend to conform to certain broad types such as the clustered or nucleated village, often with its centre of focus on route junctions. Many burghs of barony are typical examples. Such a shape could result from social or political instability, but equally could be a reflection of farming methods – the runrig system of the small proprietor type would have had a natural tendency to produce such settlements. On the other hand, the baron's territory would be dotted with 'dispersed' settlements or 'farmtouns' consisting of one or two families (such as the familiar 'kirktons' and 'miltons'). Dispersed settlements will also feature in pastoral, planned or colonized environments – market gardens or small-holdings for example. Another type of nucleated settlement was the 'linear', with the buildings in one long line along a street. This configuration has been correlated with a variety of factors including the growth of markets along major routeways, and also with strip farming (in burghs, for example, which were nearly always semi-rural with pigs running in the streets, long narrow 'tofts' were farmed to the rear of the terraced tenements). Of course, such shapes could also be determined by the physical geography of the area, or be the expression of aesthetic, economic or social theories – examples of the latter being the planned villages of the eighteenth century and the garden cities of our own era.

As settlements became larger, factors affecting their structure became more complex. In the medieval burghs, for example, it has been argued that noxious and anti-social processes such as tanning, smithing and pottery making were sometimes banished outside the gates, to a 'sub-urb'. Here, where the burgesses could not easily enforce their craft and trading monopolies, there grew up havens for the work-shy, the vagrant and the tinker. You could test the validity of this model by a study of occupations and criminal propensities in the suburbs, which will sometimes be found on the other side of a river skirting the main burgh. A general model of the same type argues that the lower a person's social class, the further he will live from the centre of the burgh. Until the advent of metalled roads not even the wealthy had much advantage in mobility over the poor in towns – everybody walked. From a later period you might like to examine how railways and cars contributed to the transformation of urban structures through the separation of the working environment from the residential quarters.

As burghs grew, various other types of suburbs developed.

'Ribbon suburbs' were located along the major route into the town –
they should include a high number of inns; 'marginal suburbs'
fronted the streets that skirted the old town walls (sometimes they
became boulevards). The better-off townspeople first abandoned
the centre when the common lands and private estates on the
periphery were developed under feuing plans drawn up by the
superior. The superior wielded many of the powers now held by
council planning departments: their feu charters (which can be
studied in sasine registers) often imposed strict conditions on the
feuars as to what use could be made of their land.

The first industrial suburbs developed at the start of the nineteenth
century, when the large and complex urban conurbations that we
know today began their evolution. Urban geography has provided
many methodological tools with which to analyse such settlements;
there is space here to mention only one or two.

It is argued that in pre-industrial towns political and religious
structures predominated at the centre, whilst in industrial towns the
shopping centre is the key element, the cause possibly being the
ability of retailers to pay the highest prices (this model sees towns as
battlefields of economic forces). The industrial economy that first
differentiated the retailer from the producer can be monitored by the
growth of warehousing, which is indicative of the presence of the
wholesaler – a key figure in industrial society, which basically
involves the domination of a market from an ever more distant
location.

A second model from urban geography identifies 'fixation lines'
within the city. These are natural lines of demarcation – originally
physical boundaries such as old town walls, but later perimeters
established by the cycles of growth and slump in the building
industry (in itself an indicator of the level of economic activity). On
the further side of a fixation line, a fringe belt pushed ever outwards
in waves, with hospitals, asylums, schools and sewage works at one
time on the rim (as being uncompetitive services in profit terms)
becoming sucked into the urban fabric. Parks and playing fields can
be seen as isolated islands of original green belt. You could make a
study of such areas in your locality to discover how and why they
were preserved. As well as growth outwards, there is constant
pressure on the existing urban core for redevelopment to meet new
needs, the successive stages of an inner city housing suburb
described in the last chapter forming part of the process. You could
look at the history of such a suburb in the light of the economic
pressures upon it, bearing in mind that in addition to the question of
land use – which is relatively flexible – there are two more
conservative elements in the landscape. These are, first, the plan or
layout of the suburb which can often preserve features several
hundred years old; and secondly its architecture, which is also
conservative, though less so than the plan. One possible topic for

study would be the adaptation of local buildings through time in response to the demands made of them.

Communications

Maps can be used for studying the relationship between settlements as well as for their structure. Central-place theory argues that the landscape is structured as a hierarchy of centres for goods and services, ranging from local immediate needs – food for example – to specialized requirements which will be satisfied at a larger but probably more distant centre. The resulting pattern in the landscape approximates to a hexagonal mesh, which is (in mathematical terms) the optimal shape for interlocking units. As a possible topic you could look at the goods and services offered in your local community over the last two hundred years or so, identifying key centres and changes in local provision.

The relationship among settlements is also indicated by the lines of communication among them. Six different types of pattern have been identified, from the centre-oriented (radial routes from one settlement to dependent settlements) and the branching network (the shortest path connecting all points) to an unstructured route connecting all points in turn. Conclusions can be drawn accordingly about the economic importance of historic settlements – the unstructured pattern for instance will suggest a basically subsistence economy.

The first representation of roads on a Scottish map occurs on Pont's *Map of Lothian and Linlitquo* 1610. Other early sources of information are the records of the Privy Council and archaeological studies. Roads were of primitive construction until the second half of the seventeenth century, when coaches were first introduced. In response to the ensuing pressure for improvement, statute labour was instituted in 1669, under the aegis of the commissioners of supply and justices of the peace, the 'tenants, cottars and other labouring men' being bound to maintain the roads. The measure was hardly popular – in the words of Ann E. Whetstone (1981), 'ten hours work per day for three days twice a year on roads which might be miles from their homes could have held little attraction for anyone'. In the eighteenth century, further powers were given to the commissioners and justices, both of whose archives will be relevant in the study of the subject. There were still deficiencies in the system, however, which led to the development of two alternatives: the commutation of statute labour for taxation, and the turnpike system, whereby private operators built and maintained roads on which tolls were charged. Some schemes adopted features of both, and in all cases a private act of Parliament was required for their introduction, as a consequence of which plans were supplied and are held in the House of Lords Record Office. They are listed in volume two of the *Early Maps of Scotland* mentioned on page 115. Where commutation took place, road trustees were appointed for each district of the county (sometimes parish) and their minute books will be found with the archives of the commissioners of supply (the trustees were usually chosen from among their members). Statutes of 1823 and 1831 consolidated private turnpike acts, and statute labour was virtually abolished in 1845.

In the eighteenth century, mapmakers progressively gave the representation of roads a higher priority; indeed, some maps were produced specifically in connection with road surveying (for example the Highland surveys carried out for General Wade 1725–35). More widespread travel also led to a demand for guides and route maps, pioneer examples being Andrew Armstrong, *Bowles's New Pocket Map of Scotland* . . . 1775, and George Taylor and Andrew Skinner's *Taylor and Skinner's Survey and Maps of the Roads of North Britain or Scotland*, 1776. George Taylor was also responsible for a manuscript roadbook, *Sketches of the Roads of Scotland*, 1785 which is held in Cambridge University Library.

From this period Highland roads are particularly well documented. The Forfeited Estate Papers are a good source, whilst in 1803 there was appointed a special commission for Highland roads and bridges. Much of the early surveying was carried out by Thomas Telford, and in all about 1000 miles of road and over 1000 bridges were constructed. The annual reports of the commission, held in the Scottish Record Office (E330), include maps of routes under construction. The Scottish Record Office has produced a source list for roads, as has the National Register of Archives in respect of privately held papers.

Nineteenth-century roads can be investigated through the papers of the Lord Advocate's office and the *Report of the Royal Commission for Inquiring into Matters Relating to the Public Roads of Scotland*, 1860. An act of 1878 abolished turnpikes, and all major roads and bridges became the responsibility of county road boards which were agencies of the county road trustees (joint bodies comprising commissioners of supply and representatives of ratepayers and town councils). In 1889 the county road boards were subsumed under the new county councils, which remained the bodies responsible until 1975, except for trunk roads which were successively transferred to the control of the Ministry of Transport and the secretary of state for Scotland (Scottish Development Department).

Roads were the principal means of internal trade and communication until the late eighteenth century, when canals entered their brief period of glory. Surviving canal records are the subject of a Scottish Record Office source list and of an article by Charles Hadfield, 'Sources for the History of British Canals', *Journals of Transport History*, volume 2, no. 2, November 1955, pp. 80–9.

It was, however, the railway which caused the greater impact in the long run, and the development of many a settlement in the mid nineteenth century can be linked to its arrival. The establishment of a railway also required an act of Parliament, and the House of Lords Record Office contains plans for those for which an application was made – more than were actually built – a topic which could be pursued, particularly in the case of some of the more bizarre proposals. More than 10,000 railway plans are held in the Scottish Record Office, including drawings of specific station buildings, and collections are also to be found in the National Library of Scotland and Aberdeen University Library. The British Rail archives, deposited with the Scottish Record Office, include the archives of the private companies taken over at nationalization, details of the holdings being given in the *Annual Report of the Keeper of the Records for 1969*. Most Scottish companies have been the subject of monographs published by David & Charles, though these emphasize the technical aspects rather than the social and economic.

Tramways, like railways, made possible the zoning of an urban environment. As a possible study, you could assess the changing structure of a town which followed from the introduction of a tramway system. Town councils were involved in the establishment of tramways. This was one area – others were gas and water supply –where local acts of Parliament were originally necessary in that the councils concerned had no statutory powers covering these undertakings. However, because of the unwieldiness of the system of local acts, various general statutes were passed (Gas and Water Facilities Act 1870, Tramways Act 1870, General Piers and Harbours Act 1861), which introduced a system of *provisional orders* granted by the Board of Trade. The legislation was extended to include all extra-statutory council undertakings by the Private Legislation Procedure (Scotland) Act 1899, under which applications were made to the secretary for Scotland for provisional orders, based on *draft provisional orders* submitted to him. The introduction of extra-statutory services often sharply divided the local community (referenda were often held), and interesting studies can be made of relevant council minutes, local newspapers and the campaign literature for and against. The last-named can often be found in local history library collections. Similar controversies often surrounded the implementation of acts which were 'adoptive' rather than compulsory, such as the public library acts.

Place names

Maps are an important source of information for place names, which linguists can use to throw light on the origin and functions of settlements. There is scope for field work here, though you are advised first to consult the place name records held by the School of Scottish Studies to avoid duplicating its already considerable researches. Its collection includes almost a million historical and current place names, plus 500 tapes of information recorded in the field and related to annotated 1:10,560 Ordnance Survey maps. Another important source is the object name books (1856–1982) kept by Ordnance Survey field workers, in which were recorded local views on names and their origins. Even specific house names are included. Microform copies of the name books are kept by the National Monuments Record, the frail originals being deposited in the Scottish Record Office.

Though the amateur can do useful work in establishing the origin and pattern of names of fields, buildings and streets, he should beware of becoming involved in etymological studies of older settlement names unless he is a specialist in linguistics. Scottish libraries are littered with pseudoscientific works on etymology, but such works cannot in the main be taken too seriously. Etymology is an exacting science and the evolution of place names is constrained within strict laws governing possible sound groupings and changes. A work to consult for background information is W. F. H. Nicolaisen, *Scottish Place Names: Their Study and Significance* (Batsford, 1976, reissued with corrections, 1986).

Land ownership

In any study of a settlement, the history of its ownership will need to be established at an early stage – many records, particularly agricultural ones, are to be found among private papers, and those which are relevant will need to be identified.

As we have seen, the early administration of Scottish localities was the responsibility of barons, so named because they held their feus direct from the crown. The word 'baron' itself had varying significance at different times, and became somewhat devalued after the emergence of a nobility based on title in the later Middle Ages. Titles were symptomatic of a new emphasis on class, and a strict ranking developed, the ranks being, in order of precedence, dukes, marquesses, earls (this an ancient Scottish title, married to more recent influences from chivalry), viscounts and lords (another term which went through various permutations in meaning, eventually becoming synonymous with baron). Titles, unlike baronies, were not linked to specific territories and some nobles, together with their cadet branches, built up huge land holdings from one end of Scotland to the other. It is often the case, therefore, that important maps and records concerning your parish form part of muniments or estate papers of an aristocratic family whose main seat may not even be in your region.

It must be remembered that the number of people who owned land (or to be more strictly accurate 'held feus') was very limited. T. C. Smout (1970) estimated that in about 1600, apart from the south west where small estates were common, a mere 5000 men 'possessed the right to inherit or sell the ground they held'. Chief among these were around 100 nobles and Highland chiefs, and beneath them in the feudal hierarchy smaller landowners loosely known as 'lairds'. Together they comprised the heritors. Smaller proprietors in the south west were known as 'bonnet lairds' and elsewhere there were a small number of owner-occupiers called 'feuars' or 'portioners'. Two important groups of tenants were 'wadsetters' (creditors of a landowner enjoying use of the estate) and 'tacksmen', often relatives of major landowners who leased large chunks of territory from them, especially in the Highlands, where the practice has been seen as an element of the clan system. Tenants generally could farm quite substantial territories; they also served on agricultural 'courts associated with baronies. These were known as 'birlaw' or 'boorlaw' courts, which died out in most cases in the eighteenth century. The landless classes comprised, in order of decreasing social status, tenants (sometimes called 'husbandmen' or 'gudemen'), crofters, cottars and farm labourers.

Ownership can often be established through a study of existing parish histories. For eighteenth-century times and later, heritors' records will indicate the landowners in your area, though the statistical accounts also generally give this information. Earlier owners can be traced through the *Register of the Great Seal* (sometimes called by its Latin title *Registrum Magni Sigilli*) which has been published in 11 volumes covering 1306–1668. It recorded charters of grants of land, confirmations and commissions to major offices. Most of the charters are in Latin, but you can identify the beneficiaries and territories concerned through indexes of person and place. If you want to develop skills in reading charters, consult Cosmo Innes, *Scotch Legal Antiquities*, Edmonston & Douglas, 1872. The *Register of the Privy Seal* (published for the years 1488–1584) consists of minor grants and commissions in the main, though it includes some charters not to be found in the Register of the Great Seal. The *Register of Tailzies* (or Entails) was mentioned in the last chapter in connection with the register of improvements on entailed estates. It is useful for tracing the changing ownership of estates burdened by entail, though it is an unpublished register (held in the Scottish Record Office). Other property registers mentioned in the last chapter, particularly the registers of sasines, also include details of sales and mortgages of estates.

The history of the noble families and their ramifications is expounded in a series of major family histories commissioned in the nineteenth century. These are all listed in Joan P. S. Ferguson, *Scottish Family Histories Held in Scottish Libraries*, Scottish Central Library, 1960 (new edition pending from the National Library of Scotland), and those covering local families should be available in your local history library. The standard work on the aristocracy as a whole is James Balfour Paul, *The Scots Peerage*, David Douglas, 1904–14 (nine volumes).

Specific details of size and location of estates can be obtained through three surveys spanning two centuries. L. P. Timperley, *Directory of Landownership in Scotland circa 1770*, Scottish Record Society, 1976 gives the valuation of estates only. Much more detailed was the contemporary survey *Return of Owners of Land and Heritages in Scotland 1872–3*, HMSO, 1874. The third survey is cartographic – a mapping of Scottish estates carried out in the late 1960s by Roger Millman. The maps are held by the Scottish Record Office and form the basis of the work of John McEwen, *Who Owns Scotland?*, EUSPB, 1977 which gives rough acreages of most estates. Current acreages are difficult to establish – for research purposes you may be able to acquire relevant information from the Scottish Landowners Federation, 18 Abercromby Place, Edinburgh EH3 6LB.

Genealogical data on landowning families are to be found in John Bernard Burke, *Genealogical and Heraldic Dictionary of the Peerage and Baronetage of the British Empire*, which has appeared in numerous editions over the last hundred years or so, the latest being 1970, and its rival *Debrett's Peerage* which last appeared in 1985. Both include baronets, a later addition to the titled ranks introduced by James VI, and knights. The lesser gentry can be investigated in John Bernard Burke, *A Genealogical and Heraldic Dictionary of the Landed Gentry of Great Britain and Ireland*, which has likewise appeared in many editions.

Agriculture

For several thousand years the cultivation of crops, together with the later development of animal domestication, was the most important influence on settlement patterns and land use – indeed, this has only ceased to be the case in the last 200 years or so. Every area of Scotland has been affected, even the barren moorlands of the Highlands and Borders, but the specific practices adopted in any locality have depended upon the terrain and soil in the context of the technology available at any time, as well as on economic factors. In respect of the latter you might like to consider a model of Von Thünen which relates choice of farming methods to the distance of the farm from major markets. The result is concentric zones around centres of settlement – with market gardening close to the centre (because of intensive labour needs, highest transport costs and the perishable nature of the goods). Traditionally, an inner zone would have been devoted to wood production – at one time wood was of paramount importance for fuel. Each concentric zone results from the choice of an optimal strategy for the farmer, based on production and transport costs and land values, the outermost zones being given over to the least intensive activities in terms both of land use and of transport costs – cattle grazing for example.

The early history of Scottish agriculture has been illuminated by modern techniques of archaeology, through analysis of carbonized grain, pollen and artefacts found on prehistoric sites. The earliest historical sources are cartularies, rental books and collections of estate writs, by means of which farm management techniques can be investigated. The records of monastic houses, pioneers of many agricultural innovations, are particularly valuable in this respect, for their standard and extent of record keeping exceeded that found elsewhere. Most of the records have been published by the various publishing societies. Barony and birlaw court records are a fruitful source for the sixteenth to eighteenth centuries: they deal with matters such as neighbourhood disputes, illegal woodcutting and compulsory labour on the 'home farm' (i.e. that farmed by the landowner or major tenant – identifiable through the farm name 'mains' which is a corruption of the Norman 'demesne'). For lands held by the crown, there is information to be gleaned from the *Exchequer Rolls* (see page 135) about revenues, crop yields, tenure and regulations for husbandry. Of similar import are the registers of testaments (see pp. 97–8), which include inventories of stock, crops and implements. Tacks and other rental arrangements were often recorded in registers of deeds (see pp. 129–30), and also survive in estate papers from the seventeenth century (of course, they were often thrown away after their expiry).

For the age of agricultural improvement, there is a dramatic increase in the number of sources available. Estate maps have already been discussed, but there are also many surviving estate archives, including letters, records of improving experiments and factors' account books. In addition there are many published accounts, including the statistical accounts which have already been discussed (they are a mine of information about farming life) and two county-based surveys carried out by the Board of Agriculture, for which volumes (two for each county) were published between 1793 and 1816. A list of these, plus a complete bibliography of other contemporary accounts, experiments and surveys is given in J. A. Symon, *Scottish Farming, Past and Present*, Oliver & Boyd, 1959. Forfeited estate papers should not be neglected – they can provide a picture of change over the hundred or so years from 1716 to 1824. The same century also saw attempts to stimulate the Scottish economy, and much of the effort went into the linen industry, linked to home-grown flax. The relevant records are those of the Board of Manufactures (from 1727) held in the Scottish Record Office (extracts have been published by the Scottish History Society).

Farming improvements encouraged the production of pro-gressive journals such as the *Farmer's Magazine* 1801–25 which gave detailed quarterly reports on the agriculture of different counties.

The *Transactions of the Royal Highland and Agricultural Society* (originally published as *prize essays*) form a continuous series from the late eighteenth century to the present day. The society was one of many agricultural associations which blossomed at the time – records of many others are held by the National Library of Scotland.

Regular statistical information is available from 1866, when the first agricultural census (based on parish) was taken. Since that time, the census has been repeated annually, and can be used to plot developments in local farming methods. Researchers are sometimes disappointed in not being able to obtain statistical information for specific farms – such data are very difficult to come by in most cases, as the Department of Agriculture's statistics are based only on a cross-section of typical returns. Those engaged in current or comparative study can receive some assistance from the Intelligence Branch of the Department of Agriculture in Edinburgh.

The parish censuses form part of the Department of Agriculture's archive in the Scottish Record Office, and the researcher would do well to consult this inventory in some detail. It includes the records of the Congested Districts Board 1897–1911, set up to distribute government aid, and the Board of Agriculture 1911–29, the predecessor of the Department. Other official nineteenth-century sources are the registers of improvements on entailed estates and the papers of the Lord Advocate's Department, collected as background material in the drafting of legislation. County newspapers date from the mid nineteenth century in the main, and are also a most valuable source for the agricultural historian.

Traditional farming life has received a lot of attention latterly. Researchers could make use of oral records from the School of Scottish Studies and material from the Country Life Archive at the National Museum of Antiquities and farming museum at Ingliston. Many monographs of varying quality have investigated similar themes, which can also be explored through the novels of such writers as Lewis Grassic Gibbon.

Crofting papers (from 1866) include the records of the Crofters Commission and its successor the Scottish Land Court. A Commission of Enquiry into Crofting Conditions 1950–55 led to the establishment of a new Crofters' Commission to reorganize the crofting system. A Scottish Record Office source list is relevant: Number 26 (Highlands and Islands) – it includes *Sources for Crofting Disturbances 1883–6*.

Trade and industry

In medieval times the local economy was in large measure a subsistence one, based on small market centres (such as burghs of barony). Most economic activity was agriculturally dependent or related and carried on by craftsmen such as smiths, wrights, tanners, baxters (bakers), cordiners (shoemakers), fleshers and lorimers (harness makers). The scale of such an economy was dictated by distances that could be walked in a day – only pedlars and merchants from the royal burghs ventured any further in the pursuit of trade. This pattern can be contrasted with an industrial economy such as we know today, in which the size of settlements and employment patterns are no longer related to the economic activity in the surrounding countryside – rather the reverse. The industrial revolution has had a greater impact on human settlement patterns than any other factor since crops were first grown approximately 10,000 years ago.

The contrast between the two ways of life must not be over-emphasized, however, for even before the growth of towns – in the sixteenth and seventeenth centuries – the Scottish agrarian economy was no longer based entirely on subsistence (if, indeed, it ever had been totally). There was for example a traditional interdependence of lowlands and highlands, the surplus grain produce of the one being traded for the livestock (cattle) of the other. In fact, the growth of the grain trade in the seventeenth century and the concomitant increase in the size of markets has been a process identified by historians as marking the transition from a medieval to a modern economic system.

There are three ways of investigating economic activity: through the affairs of an individual, in the history of particular firms or industries, and by a consideration of macro-economic factors such as trade and growth.

The affairs of an individual

References to an individual's economic situation have been made already in connection with *cessio bonorum* processes and sasine registers. His level of prosperity or standard of living can be investigated in many similar types of material – wills, inventories of moveable estate and valuation rolls, as well as through diaries and household accounts. Such studies should generally contain a comparative element – prosperity needs to be gauged against that of contemporaries. In this respect, it is difficult to separate altogether a study of the individual from the macro-economic circumstances of his time (comparative economic studies present problems for the local historian, as will be seen below). On safer ground, we can look at excessive manifestations of prosperity in the form of the great mansions of the eighteenth and nineteenth centuries. From where did the money come to build these houses? Often it was from outside the locality if not from overseas; in which circumstances one could study the impact of the influx of such wealth on the local community. Another topic which could be pursued is the opportunities open to persons of different social class at different times, and the related subject of mobility. How often did people move house or jobs? Burgess registers and estate leases and feus can be used in this study.

A group of registers not hitherto considered can be used to answer many of the questions about individual economic relationships. Notable among these is the *Register of Deeds*, known technically as the *Books of Council and Session* and dating from 1554. It serves all three functions of a public register – execution, preservation and publication – and as a consequence its contents are varied, including even, for example, duplicate entries of records in registers of sasines, as well as bonds, protests (for which see page 130) and wills. Indeed, it has been claimed by J. M. Thomson (1922) that

From the Register of Deeds, it is hard to say what one may not learn. We may find there unexpectedly the contract for the building of a historic bridge, or a historic castle; or, it may be, the setting up of a parish school, with details of the modest inducements offered to the first schoolmaster; or the contract for the building of a church or the purchase of a peal of bells; or an arrangement between the patron of a living and his presentee, sometimes of a very dubious character; or an agreement between neighbours for draining a bog or setting up a race meeting; or a contract for raising a regiment of Scotsmen for service in a foreign country.

The Register of Deeds arose from the practice of presenting deeds to the Court of Session (deeds are any written agreement) or other courts for the purpose of having them registered in the court books, thus preserving 'authentic evidence of their terms and at the same time, by the consent of parties, obtaining for the deeds so recorded, the force of actual decree or judgement of the court'. Duplicate entries of deeds are even found in the courts' registers of acts and decrees, for the deed became an act, being retained by the clerk of court as warrant (see page 44).

Originally the custom was to register deeds not only with the Court of Session but also in the books of every sheriff court, commissary court and even burgh and regality courts. This was to ensure widespread publication, but such a procedure became unwieldy, and an act of 1685 withdrew from the inferior courts right of registration except in cases where execution was to occur within their jurisdictions. In 1809 the burgh and commissary court registers of deeds were further reduced in scope, leaving the sheriff courts and Court of Session as the main bodies responsible.

The Court of Session deeds are in three series, the first covering the years 1554–1657, the second 1661–1811 and the third from 1812. Use of the second series is handicapped by the parallel arrangement under the names of the three clerks' offices – Dalrymple, Durie and Mackenzie. As in the case of other court records, minute books are for some periods the only finding aids, but in the present case use can be made of an indexed manuscript calendar of deeds for the years 1554–95 (in the Scottish Record Office) and published name indexes for the years 1661–95, 1750–53, 1765–9 and from 1770 onwards. Work on the period between 1695 and 1750 continues.

We have seen that one of the most important functions of registers of deeds is to give legal sanction to agreements, bonds and contracts; the necessity of such sanctions in any developed economy is obvious. On this basis has arisen a range of further registers to regulate and enforce the law relating to creditors and debtors, the recourses available to the former constituting in some respects a procedural chain up to and including the bankruptcy of the debtor.

A first stage is a 'protest' whereby a creditor is granted a certificate when a bill of exchange (roughly speaking an I.O.U.) has not been honoured. Originally protests were recorded in the registers of deeds (hence the latter are sometimes known as registers of deeds and protests). In 1812, however, a separate Register of Protests was established.

Creditor/debtor relationships come under the area of law known as *diligence*, one aspect of which is the process whereby a creditor takes steps to force a debtor to appear in court, to give security and to obey a decree already made by the court. The origin of the practice lies in the lack of provision in Scots civil law for enforcing court decisions. In some early cases bonds contained clauses whereby the debtor submitted himself to the jurisdiction of a church court – if he defaulted, he was liable to excommunication. In the king's courts, an equally dramatic procedure was used – that of 'horning', by which the defaulter's identity was broadcast by the blowing of a hunting horn, and he could be pursued and killed by anyone who chose. A less drastic fate – forfeiture of one's entire property – was a later development of horning. A third method of enforcement was 'poinding', which authorized the 'distraint' (seizure) of moveable property to the value of the debt only. The goods remained in the ownership of the debtor, but he was debarred from disposing of them. 'Arrestment' was related: it prevented a third party from making over moveable property to the debtor even though it was owed to him, the intention being, as with poinding, to freeze the assets of the debtor. Both poinding and arrestment were actions brought to the court by individual creditors (they are still competent).

Various registers have been kept by the Court of Session and sheriff courts to record these various proceedings. Registers of hornings were kept by sheriff courts and the Court of Session, as were registers of inhibitions. 'Inhibition' was a means of preventing a debtor making away with his land and goods even though no decree had as yet been obtained against him (for which reason it was always necessary to check the register before registering sasines). Particular registers of inhibitions were maintained by the sheriff courts up to 1868, since which time only the general register has continued, though combined with other registers (see below).

Sequestration, introduced in 1772, marked a stage in the liberalization of debtor/creditor law – as we saw in Chapter Three, sequestration could avert the imprisonment of the debtor. It involves taking over his assets for division among the creditors as a whole, and as such takes precedence over most personal diligence as outlined above. Sequestration applies to individuals and partnerships, but not companies. Sequestration forms part of bankruptcy proceedings, which are complex, and the use of records is facilitated by a Scottish Record Office typescript *Introduction to the Law of Bankruptcy Relating to Sequestrations 1772–1913*. West Register House holds an *Alphabetical List of Sequestrated Bankrupts 1839–1913*.

Under sequestration proceedings, the assets are taken over by trustees representing the creditors, and their minute books (CS 96 – Bill Chamber Productions) held in West Register House include valuable inventories of the bankrupts' effects. Petitions for sequestration were recorded in the Register of Adjudications (formerly the Register of Apprisings). This register was combined with the Register of Inhibitions in 1924 to form a single register covering personal and collective diligence.

History of a business

In the study of local commerce and industry, the first task is to identify the relevant companies in your locality. You could, of course, study your own firm or other still current enterprises, but if you want to investigate older businesses, information can be found in the statistical accounts and in David Bremner, *The Industries of Scotland: Their Rise, Progress and Present Condition*, Black, 1869 (facsimile reprint by David & Charles, 1969). Ordnance Survey maps and valuation rolls also indicate factories and workshops.

A starting point in all areas of business research is to find out whether archives have been preserved. Sometimes they will still be held by the firm concerned, and permission may be granted to make use of them. If the firm no longer exists or if it does not retain its older files, enquiry should be made of the National Register of Archives or the Scottish Business Archives Council c/o Department of Economic History, Adam Smith Building, University of Glasgow G12 8RT. Collections of business archives are held by the Scottish Record Office (mainly in the GD inventory) and some can be identified by means of a source list of business archives. Important collections are also held by university archives and the National Library of Scotland.

Early industrial enterprise was usually on a small scale – mills for example. Tenants were usually obliged to have their meal ground in the landowner's mill – a burden known as 'thirlage'. The 'multure' was the toll paid to the miller – a character who frequently appears unfavourably in folk literature. Information about mills may be found among estate papers such as rental books, and the courses of mill lades can sometimes be traced in the modern landscape – in some cases, different technological generations can be represented on the same stretch of water. Industrial sites from all ages can be investigated through industrial archaeology, a subject already discussed in the last chapter. The Scottish Society for Industrial Archaeology, c/o the Museum of Transport, 25 Albert Drive, Glasgow G41 2PE aims to 'study and record buildings, other structures and machinery illustrating the evolution of enterprises'.

There were a few major industrial projects in early times, mainly extraction industries (coal, lead, lime) and ancillary industries which exploited the by-products (salt panning, soap and glass manufacture, pottery). Originally, rights over mineral extraction or promotion of industrial enterprises were granted as monopolies to individuals or religious houses through royal charters (recorded in the Register of the Great Seal or Register of the Privy Seal) or through private acts of Parliament. In the seventeenth century, when the government gave more positive encouragement, joint-stock companies were created, application in some cases being made through the Privy Council or a Committee of Trade of the Estates of Parliament.

After the Union, active government assistance was channelled through the Board of Manufactures (1727–1847), which fostered the linen trade in particular. It was organized as a cottage industry (the hand-loom weavers became a radical force in Scottish society), but its straitened circumstances in the face of competition from the fully industrialized cotton industry at the start of the nineteenth century led to the investigation of the Select Committee on Hand Loom Weavers in 1834. Select committees were one of several governmental bodies with functions similar to those of royal commissions. Some departmental reports form long series which are particularly relevant to the subject in hand – examples are the reports of the Mines Inspectorate and Factory Inspectorate.

The growth of the industrial economy was hampered by inadequacies in company law, owing partly to the panic reaction to the South Sea Bubble crisis – the so-called Bubble Act was passed in 1719. The act placed restrictions on the establishment of incorporated bodies, crown charters or private acts of Parliament once again becoming a prerequisite. The degree to which this legislation affected Scotland, however, has been the subject of debate, for the situation here was complicated by differences of interpretation between English and Scots law.

Campbell (1967) argues that the position in Scotland was superior in two respects. First, some rights of granting incorporation had traditionally been vested in town councils, who could confer a 'seal of cause', on groups of craftsmen for example, and later also on charitable foundations and business enterprises. Secondly, and more important, the Scots law of partnership (i.e. for *unincorporated* groups) was more favourable to businesses. In English law, Campbell argues that 'the law of partnership failed to recognize the distinct *persona* of the firm, so that no matter how large an unincorporated joint-stock company became, legally it remained no more than an aggregate of individuals'.

In Scots law, partnership, even when unincorporated, involved a concept of legal personality, and three important consequences flowed from this interpretation, all of which gave unincorporated bodies many of the advantages supposedly reserved for incorporations. They were, first, the transferability of shares, secondly, limited liability for the shareholders (in partnerships of the English type all partners were jointly and severally liable for all the debts of the company), and thirdly, the legal personality of the firm, which allowed it to enter into litigation as an entity.

Progressively, the English interpretation came to prevail, even in Scottish courts, and by the early nineteenth century business development was being severely restricted. The shortcomings were removed by a series of statutes passed at that time, the most important being the Registration Act of 1844 by which companies could be formed through a simple process of registration, and acts of 1856 and 1862 which introduced the concept of limited liability.

Under the new system, companies are registered at the Companies Registration Office, 102 George Street, Edinburgh EH2 3DJ, where the records held include the company's memorandum of association and articles of association (i.e. its constitution), its annual reports and accounts and information about any changes in its directors or capital flotation. The Registration Office also has an index for tracing pre-1844 companies. Files of dissolved companies are passed to the Scottish Record Office (West Register House – inventory BT). Here a card index lists the companies alphabetically; this can also be used in some measure as a place index, in that many companies include a town's name as the first element of their title. These files are a valuable source for the local historian – they give a detailed picture of the business development of even quite minor communities from the mid nineteenth century in enterprises as localized as small breweries or gas works.

Patents are another useful source. They can be granted to individuals or to companies, either for new products and processes, or for improvements to existing ones. The Patent Office was set up in 1852 and is the sole office for the United Kingdom. There are two main groups of records – patent specifications and patent abstracts, the first of which are detailed descriptions of the invention, and the latter résumés of their main features. The Science Reference Library (part of the British Library in London) holds copies of all patents, but substantial collections are held by the provincial patent libraries (in Scotland the Glasgow Public Library). Patent information centres (Edinburgh and Aberdeen Public Libraries) have indexes and guidance material. Patent searching is a difficult task, and often it is best to use professional searchers, names of whom are held in the Science Reference Library. Local patent agents are listed in the *Yellow Pages* (an annual register is available from the Chartered Institute of Patent Agents, Staple Inn Buildings, London WC1V 7PZ).

For the period before the establishment of the Patent Office, the position is slightly more complicated. Prior to 1707 the right to use an invention could be granted by the sovereign, Privy Council or Parliament, but such rights did not differ from other types of monopoly such as the trading or mineral extraction rights considered above. After the Union, patents were usually recorded with the United Kingdom series (which dates back to 1617) but could also be subsequently recorded in a section of the Register of the Great Seal known as the *Paper Register*, and after 1813 in a separate *Record of Specifications*. The Scottish Record Office (West Register House) holds these specifications and also a *Calendar of Scottish Patents and Specifications 1712–1812*.

Economic history

A third possible approach to economic matters is to consider the development of a town or district in general terms, with assessments of the extent of economic activity – both trade and manufacturing – at different junctures in its history. Such a study presents greater difficulties than those discussed in the foregoing sections, in that the historian is dependent upon a partial surviving record, which precludes the use of sophisticated statistical methods commonly used in contemporary economic studies. The model developed by Rostow mentioned above, for example, argues that a growth rate of two per cent per annum is a threshold above which the economy takes off into 'self-sustaining growth'. The historian, however, is not in a position to calculate the gross national product for any year in the eighteenth century, nor any of the other major pointers such as the retail price index. He cannot produce these figures for Scotland as a whole, let alone any locality within it. Furthermore, he would be hard pressed to produce local figures even for today, for despite our preoccupation with statistics, most series are compiled from sample data and cannot give a true picture of local variation. In the study of economic activity, therefore, the local historian cannot seek to emulate the economist and must restrict himself to trying to capture the flavour of an era.

A good starting point is the customs accounts of different ports preserved in the Exchequer records (E) and covering the seventeenth to nineteenth centuries. They can be used for establishing what goods were being produced for export; and in turn what levels of expectation were being satisfied by imported goods. For more modern periods, the variety and quantity of goods manufactured and traded in the economy can be studied through the traffic notebooks of railway companies. Newspaper advertisements will reflect changing expectations, and you could also study where the advertised good were being made. If they were coming from outside the locality, what was the effect on the local economy and why was it unable to provide the same goods competitively?

Up to the seventeenth century, trade and craft manufacture was virtually confined to the burghs. Ports were originally attached to royal burghs, who claimed a monopoly on overseas trade (sometimes ports were several miles from the towns which controlled them). The crown encouraged their development, as customs dues were one of the few means available for increasing tax revenues. Information about these ports can be found in town council minutes; and their later history, in the nineteenth century, can be traced through local acts of Parliament and subsequently provisional orders (see page 122). By the seventeenth century, however, though in theory trade remained a monopoly of royal burghs, their power was greatly weakened, and charters were granted to landowning entrepreneurs such as coal barons to erect ports, sometimes in conjunction with rights to erect burghs of barony. Later, harbours were built for the promotion of the fishing industry, which was always an important component in the Scottish economy. A Fishery Board was established in 1809 (its records form part of the Department of Agriculture archive) and its records include harbour plans, as do those of the Commission for Highland Roads and Bridges, the British Fisheries Society (GD9), British Railway and Scottish Development Department.

The level of internal trade can be studied through the *Exchequer Rolls*, which have been published in 23 volumes covering the years 1264–1600, HM Register House, 1878–1908. They contain the local accounts of sheriffs, customs officials and bailies of burghs as well as state accounts of the chamberlain of crown lands and the lord high treasurer. The accounts of the last-named official have also been published, in 13 volumes covering 1473–1580, HM Register House, 1877–1978.

An economic model that could be used in the study of burghs is the Marxist one of conflicting class interests. The elite of the burghs were the merchants who came to dominate the town councils – council minutes prominently and repeatedly feature attempts to harass and exclude 'unfreemen' from trading and manufacturing. You could make a study of this phenomenon, asking why the 'problem' persisted and to what extent the burgesses were able to control it (by the eighteenth century most of their privileges had been eroded). Another topic you could investigate is the conflict between the merchants and craftsmen of burghs. To what extent can this be understood in terms of a struggle between social classes? Many minute books of incorporations have survived from the seventeenth century onwards, and their growth can be studied. One feature was the introduction of new crafts – such as watchmaking – which in some cases led to the formation of a new incorporation, whereas in others existing incorporations widened their membership.

For more recent periods of history, study of economic development is made easier by the existence of planning literature. The first statutory recognition of local planning came with the Housing, Town Planning etc. Act 1909, whereby local authorities might draw up town planning schemes for defined areas which were liable to be developed. This and further legislation was consolidated in the Town Planning (Scotland) Act 1925 and Town and Country Planning (Scotland) Act 1932, but it was not until 1947 that the Town and Country Planning (Scotland) Act of that year obliged county councils and town councils of the larger burghs to prepare development plans to be approved by the Department of Health for Scotland. The plans included a series of surveys and reports analysing the local economy in the broader context of post-war regional survey plans (such as the Clyde Valley Plan), carried out under the aegis of regional planning advisory committees. Development plans were not, however, regarded as the final word: modifications were made to accommodate new directions, and in due course changes could be consolidated into new plans.

Since local government reorganization in 1975, there are two tiers of local government – regional councils and district councils. The former are obliged to produce regional structure plans (covering the broad infrastructure – communications, services and supplies) within which district councils must produce local plans for specific areas within their jurisdiction. Latterly, the researcher will be able to draw on much more material of the same type – annual housing reviews, conservation plans, management plans for parks and nature reserves and transport policy reviews. The third statistical accounts which have appeared over the last 30 years can be used in conjunction with this material, most of which should be held by your local history library, or failing that your district council planning department.

Population statistics are often required in connection with projects concerned with economic history, but early figures are very difficult to establish. Some calculations for medieval Scotland have been made by analysing monastic cartularies and early tax rolls. The first systematic survey was not made until 1755 by Alexander Webster, whose figures are often quoted in the statistical accounts together with figures supplied by the writer of the account. A full list of

Webster's figures is given in James Kyd, *Scottish Population Statistics*, Scottish Academic Press, 1952 (reprinted 1976). From 1801 official census figures are available, and population tables for every subsequent decade are included in the 1981 published census material. Breakdown by age and other factors for the present day is given in *Census 1981: Key Statistics for Urban Areas, Scotland*, HMSO, 1984. Population figures for parishes are straightforward, but for towns there is the problem of defining what is meant by 'a town.' In the nineteenth century, for example, royal burghs, police burghs and parliamentary burghs could all use different boundaries. You must make sure you are comparing like with like – the position can be further complicated if the burgh's boundaries were extended, resulting in an apparent sudden increase in population. Villages too are a problem, for the opposite reason that in many cases there was no local administrative unit, apart from the special district, which corresponded to villages. Technically, therefore, they would have no boundaries at all to differentiate them from the parishes in which they were situated. Nineteenth-century figures can be worked out from census enumeration books, but only if you are sure yourself where the natural boundaries lie.

Chapter Seven

WRITING AND PUBLISHING RESULTS

Writing history

At the risk of stating the obvious, still it needs to be said that the final goal of any research project, however humble, is to produce a published piece of work. The point requires emphasizing because so often the case is otherwise. Yet hopefully, from what you have read by now, you will appreciate that historical research involves a contribution to a shared pool of knowledge and ideas – and this process cannot easily take place without publication. Granted that the latter is desirable, therefore, we should now briefly examine the main obstacles to its happening.

The first problem arises from insufficient planning on the part of the researcher. It is necessary to have clearly in mind the specific historical question or questions that are being pursued – in which circumstances you can identify the moment when the questions have been answered and the project can be written up. Without such a structure there is a constant temptation to put back the day when writing begins. There is a second advantage too in the approach recommended: that the notes taken in the course of the study will already be in a semi-finished form with an ordered and logical progression which it will be relatively easy to flesh out. Contrast this with the researcher who may have collected a large amount of information but with no clear idea of its purpose or value: the result will be a dog's breakfast, and when he sits down to write, there will be nothing on which to hang an argument. It is when one is faced with a predicament of this kind that the material begins to weigh heavily and one becomes disillusioned or bored. The researcher abandons the writing, promising himself to return another day; but the vision of that wad of unorganized notes takes up residence in his imagination and he finds successive excuses for not returning to them.

Some projects are never completed because they are far too ambitious for the resources or time available to the researcher. There is a tendency to undertake a large-scale topic of unrealistic scope: even the majority of professional historians only rarely attempt a wide-ranging theme. And for the amateur, a minor project well executed is worth a thousand aborted or half-baked major projects. The scale can be very narrow indeed – perhaps the background to a single case in a sheriff court, the minute books of a single parochial board or the history of a particular street – and the conclusions reached can be couched in very provisional terms. Much of historical research is a series of tentative suggestions: the broad vision only comes from a cumulation of such propositions. So your first piece of writing need cover no more than two or three pages. Your second too may be the same, but your third can be longer, because for the first time you will be able to generalize from the knowledge you have gained from all three. The key therefore is to undertake a series of small, related projects which are written up as they are completed. Seen in this light, the prospect of publication becomes less daunting.

A third cause of reluctance in regard to publishing is modesty on the part of the historian. 'My humble work', runs the argument, 'could not possibly be of interest to others.' But if you have been following the rules of research, your work cannot but be of interest to others: a careful examination of material in the context of a well-prepared hypothesis can save another researcher in your field a great deal of time. He would otherwise have to look into the issue himself, and given the vastness of the surviving written record, especially in the last two hundred years or so, no single historian could make much progress on his own. Instead he depends upon others for well-researched articles based on primary sources.

A related argument is that you have no literary ability. This too can be dismissed: literary ability is not required. Great professional historians will have such skill – it is one aspect of their greatness – but remember that your first piece is going to be very short and that its structure has already been partly determined by the way you arrange your notes as a logical series of questions and answers. You formulated an hypothesis, you collected only that material which illuminated the problem, and you drew the conclusion. The layout of your article is already there. The best kind of historical writing has no literary pretensions at all – it is based upon being clear about the questions being asked and about making sure the reader is clear too, so that he can participate in the quest as if it were a detective novel. Purposeful writing generates its own style without the writer having to bother about it at all.

For those of you with any residual doubts, David Dymond's *Writing Local History: a Practical Guide*, Bedford Square Press, 1981 is strongly recommended. This entertaining book makes short work of pretentiousness, obfuscation and sloppiness in historical writing (as much apparent in the work of professionals as amateurs); and some of his horrendous examples can serve as a checklist of faults to be avoided against which to judge your own efforts. One or two that frequently occur can be mentioned here. The amateur is prone to exaggerate when he writes and to talk in terms wider than is justified by the context of his study. Generalization from one specific example should be avoided, as should the vague or unsupported statement – unsubstantiated assumptions or guesses generally prove to be false. Avoid self-importance, the use of the first person and other personal intrusions (do not put forward opinions, for instance). One important rule is to be honest: we can all remember the school or college examination in which we did not know the answer and spent two pages trying to pretend we did. It fooled nobody then, and it will fool nobody now. The tricks are all very familiar: glossing over a point which is obscure to us, bolstering a banal observation by the use of unnecessary jargon, or knowledge-ably talking about an author whom we have not read except at second hand in somebody else's book. In this latter connection a common trick is to use quotations from primary sources in such a way as to suggest that the originals have been read, whereas the quotations have been culled from other secondary sources. You can soon compile an impressive list of references in this way, but the content of your piece will not impress at all. The remedy is to keep your writing simple, call a spade a spade and be honest about what you do not know and what you have not studied. Do not dress up a simple argument to make it appear more profound or complex, and do not introduce irrelevant material to show off the extent of your knowledge. The integrity of your writing, if such rules are followed, will invite greater confidence in your validity as an historian than whole volumes of portentous obscurantism or jargon-ridden mumbo-jumbo.

A final piece of advice is that you put away your finished piece for at least two or three weeks after completing it. Then take it out and look at it again – it is surprising how many badly argued points or errors of grammar you will spot when you consider it afresh.

Of crucial importance, as has been suggested, is an orderly progression through the announcement of the theme or problem being discussed, the marshalling of supporting evidence and the drawing of a conclusion. The presentation of an argument in this form brings us to a key point: proper documentation of the sources being used. One can hardly overemphasize the importance of giving references, and yet there are still far too many local history publications which dispense with them altogether. An historian who does not provide them in his written work can have no excuse in today's climate of rigorous scientific discipline in all areas of knowledge.

In Chapter One details were given of the correct method of recording book, journal and archival sources. In this chapter, the problem to be considered is how to incorporate references into the written text. For this purpose it can be helpful to draw a distinction between a direct attribution and a background source. The first is specific: it will be either a quotation from another work (primary or secondary) or a statement of fact which you intend to take on trust. Such references are called *citations* and they allow your arguments to be independently checked. The second kind of reference is more general: it indicates the background reading which has helped to mould your outlook or given you ideas. Because citations relate to specific parts of your text, they must in one form or another be made in the body of the writing; general sources can be relegated to the end of the article or chapter or the book as a whole. The latter pose no problem, but citations have to be handled more carefully because of the danger of cluttering the flow of your argument. Indeed, some journal articles are so full of them as to be virtually unreadable. There may (just about) be justification for this in a learned article, but such a practice would be unsuitable in most circumstances. There is a temptation to use citations for self-justification, to prove how much you have read or how many primary sources you have consulted, as if this in itself was a virtue. It is more likely, however, that over-reliance on references is an attempt to conceal the fact that the writer has no ideas.

The incorporation of citations can be managed in three ways. First, they can be reproduced in the text in full – which has the advantage that the reader does not need to look to the bottom of the page or end of the chapter to find the reference – by which time he will have lost his place and the continuity of the argument. But the disadvantage is that full bibliographical details will need to be given every time further reference is made to the same work. The second method is to use footnotes, with indication in the text by means of reference numbers. If the citation is given at the foot of the same page there are the same advantages and disadvantages as to be found in the first method, though there is a traditional practice of using phrases such as 'op. cit.' with page references to the original citation. If, however, the bibliographical details are given at the end of the article or book, there will be no need to repeat them if subsequent references are made to the same item, but once again the thread of the argument can be lost whilst the reader is busy finding their location. A third method is a compromise between the other two, and is extensively used in scientific publications. Under this system, citation is given in an abbreviated form in the text (author and date of publication only); at the end of the article or book, the full details are provided, arranged according to author subdivided by the date of publication. Such an arrangement is particularly useful in the sciences because the recent material is more likely to follow logically from reports of earlier experiments and the chronological arrangement is therefore simultaneously a systematic one. The method or methods you decide to use in any particular case will vary according to the type and extent of citations you need to make and the type of publication in which your work is appearing. As has been suggested, there are shortcomings in all the methods; it is therefore a question of picking the one which is least objectionable or using a combination of methods, as is the case in this book.

Where to publish

The simplest form of publication is to deposit a typescript of your article with your local history library, where it can be examined by other researchers. However, if you are looking for a wider audience, the first outlet to consider is your area's local history or antiquarian society journal, whose editor's address you can obtain from your local library. Other local history societies are based, not upon the locality, but upon the subject studied, some examples being given in the Further Reading and Information section of this book. Such societies usually publish journals and would welcome relevant contributions. A full list of them is maintained by the Mitchell Library in Glasgow. Academic journals are listed in David Woodworth, *Current British Journals*, 2nd edition, Library Assocation, 1973, though this work is now somewhat out of date. For recent Scottish journals, you could consult the annual *Bibliography of Scotland* (see page 31) or the National Library of Scotland's publication *Current Periodicals*. The latter is an alphabetical listing only and is limited to journals to which the National Library of Scotland subscribes.

If you are interested in writing at a more popular level, you might consider sending a contribution to your local newspaper or general magazines such as the *Scots Magazine* or *Scottish Field*. Popular magazines are listed until title and subject in the annual *Willing's Press Guide*. In such writing it may be necessary to compromise somewhat in the matter of citations, though with skill and practice references can be introduced naturally into the text without loss of popular appeal.

In the larger-scale project, such as that undertaken by a group, the written material may be too substantial to be reproduced in the form of journal articles. In these cases it is necessary to consider some form of book or booklet production. Where the projects are organized by institutions such as the Workers' Educational Association or extramural departments of universities, publication can sometimes be arranged (and financed) through the body concerned. Most libraries too now have publication programmes and may be interested in publishing your work for you.

One possibility to be considered is to undertake your own publishing programme, though it is a golden rule that publishing through an institution is always preferable to doing it on your own – if the choice is available. Publishing and marketing are skills in their own right and the beginner may be embarking on a dangerous course. Getting a work printed is simplicity itself, though expensive; but selling is another matter altogether. There is no point in producing 500 copies of a book if you cannot sell more than 100; and the frequency of this error and the unfounded optimism that causes it justifies emphasizing the warning. In particular you need to be sure of your outlets – shops, libraries and institutions – and realistic about sales prospects before you commit yourself.

Attention must be paid to design, including the cover (which should be bright and attractive), the type face and the overall unity of style. A very common mistake in amateur productions is to crowd the page with too much text – at least 50 per cent of the surface of the page should be given over to the margins at the sides and top and bottom if the page is to appear pleasing and uncluttered to the eye. Help on these and related matters, such as photographic reproduction, can be obtained from Scotland's Cultural Heritage Project, History of Medicine and Science Unit, University of Edinburgh, High School Yards, Edinburgh EH1 1LZ.

Production costs can be reduced in various ways. First, the text and layout can be prepared by yourself, using the more sophisticated type faces available with modern electric typewriters; the printing process called *offset lithography* can use plates taken directly from your copy – indeed for short runs, you can type directly on to a plate. You could also consider the possibility of subsidization, through sale of advertisement space, grants from bodies such as community councils and trusts (for which details can be found in the annual *Directory of Grant Making Trusts*) and sponsorship from local firms.

Do not think however that subsidization lets you off the hook as far as marketing is concerned. To be left with 395 unsold books out of 500 is an unsatisfactory situation irrespective of whether they have been financed by yourself or others. Your marketing strategy should start with your public library, which will probably want to buy copies direct from you and may agree to act as selling agent. If your book is likely to have a more general appeal, you should try to get approval copies accepted by library book suppliers in Scotland – your library will be able to give you the addresses. If your book is suitable for school work, you will also need to contact school book suppliers; alternatively you could circulate a publicity leaflet to history departments and school librarians (in most cases Scottish school libraries are run by the regional councils, whereas public libraries are the responsibility of the district councils).

These general ideas apart, marketing in a small community can be relatively straightforward – by word of mouth, publicity leaflets pushed through doors, or sale-or-return copies deposited with local newsagents. Where the market is larger, however, a different strategy will be necessary. Review copies can be sent out, though this is obviously an expensive method of publicity which should be used sparingly. It will be unproductive to send copies to national journals or magazines which are unlikely to be read by your prospective buyers (if, that is, your book even gets reviewed). You should concentrate rather on your local newspapers and radio stations, relevant magazines in the local history field and the widely circulated *Scots Magazine*.

For newspaper coverage, it is always best to apply the inertia principle – that the less work there is for the reporter, the greater is the likelihood that your item will be mentioned. To this end, you should include with the review copy a press release giving names and telephone numbers of two contacts together with a piece about the book and its background. The length should be so judged as to make reproduction in full a realistic option; but the item should also be written and arranged in such a way that it can easily be cut without loss of context. In other words, a brief introductory passage of essential information should be followed by paragraphs expanding on some of the points made. Press releases should be succinct and lively and exploit any unusual or 'human interest' angle.

Consideration of lively promotional material should also include the information given in the book itself. Jacket blurbs are often weak or non-existent in amateur publications, but are extremely import-ant in conveying the book's overall scope and purpose, allowing the browser to establish a definite image in his mind at the outset and enticing him to look further. A book without a blurb is more likely to be replaced on the shelf without further investigation.

It is a mistake to think that a single review will make a profound difference to sales. Marketing is a continuous process, and saturation techniques are the only means of ensuring that all potential buyers are made aware of the publication. Despite library displays, advertisements in newsagents' windows, a radio or television slot and sales drives at local fetes and jumble sales, communities manage to remain blissfully unaware of a book's existence. Such techniques must be employed over a long period of time – which brings us back to our original point: though publishing can be a rewarding experience, it must be remembered that it is a project in its own right, not an afterthought to a research project.

Once your book has been produced a copy must, by law, be deposited with the British Library, and six other copyright libraries in the country are entitled to ask for free copies. The positive side from your point of view is that it ensures the book will be recorded in the *British National Bibliography*, where it is likely to be noticed by institutional buyers. You should also record your title with *British Books in Print*, which is the principal tool used in the book trade for tracing bibliographical details. It is published by James Whitaker & Son, 12 Dyott Street, London WC1A 1DF, from whom you can also obtain a *standard book number* (a unique code identifying each book) which is used in ordering and invoicing transactions. It helps if the number can be printed into the book.

Commercial publishers have not been mentioned so far; and for most local productions they will not be a feasible proposition. Commercial publishers are in the main orientated towards national marketing and will have neither the time nor local knowledge to take on such works. Small local commercial firms or newspaper offices do sometimes publish local history books, though often they themselves have little expertise in book design and marketing. They will also be unlikely to offer editorial services – a considerable drawback, as an outside critical viewpoint is of immense value in any proposed publication. A do-it-yourself production will of course be similarly disadvantaged – which reinforces the advice already given, to investigate all the possibilities for publishing through institutional and academic outlets before embarking on your own project.

APPENDIX: Table of Local Government Functions 1832–1975: A Selective List

Bodies	General Legislation

1832–89
Town Councils
Police Commissioners 1833–
Commissioners of Supply
  Police Committees 1857–
Road Trustees
Parochial Boards 1845–
District Lunacy Boards 1857–
Special Districts (Water Supply and
  Drainage) 1867–
School Boards 1872–
Justices of the Peace	

1889–1929
County Councils 1889–
Standing Joint Committees
District Committees (larger counties
  only) 1889–
Special Districts (Water Supply and
  Drainage)
Special Districts (Lighting, etc.) 1894–
Parochial Boards –1894
Parish Councils 1894–
  Landward Committees (for landward
  part of parishes containing burghs)
District Boards of Lunacy –1913
District Boards of Control 1913–
School Boards –1918
County Secondary Education
  Committees 1892–
Education Authorities 1918–
Distress Committees 1905–
Town Councils
Police Commissioners –1900
Justices of the Peace
	Local Government (Scotland) Act 1889

Bodies	General Legislation
1929–74	Local Government (Scotland) Act 1929
County Councils	
District Councils	
(larger counties only)	
any county council function could be	
delegated except police and education	
Counties of Cities	
Town Councils (large)	
Town Councils (small)	Local Government (Scotland) Act 1947
Special Districts (those for water supply	
and drainage abolished 1949)	
Joint Committees (of County Councils,	
Town Councils and District	
Councils)	
Justices of the Peace	
1975–	Local Government (Scotland) Act 1973
Regional Councils	
District Councils (different from	
pre-1974)	
Community Councils	

Functions

Police and Environmental Services

Legislation 1832–89	Police	Lighting/paving scavenging	Water supply/ sewage
Police Act 1832	Collection of 'rogue' money from county free-holders transferred to commissioners of supply		
Police Act 1833	Powers to royal burghs and burghs of barony to raise forces	Powers to royal burghs and burghs of barony	Powers to royal burghs and burghs of barony (many schemes
Police Act 1839	Powers to commissioners of supply to raise county forces		through local acts/private water companies consolidated 1847 and 1863)
Police Act 1847	1833 powers extended to parliamentary burghs		

Legislation	Police	Lighting/paving scavenging	Water supply/ sewage
Police and Improvement (Scotland) Act 1850	1833 powers extended to police burghs (minimum population 1200)		
Police (Scotland) Act 1857	All counties and some burghs *obliged* to introduce police (town councils in burghs; commissioners of supply in counties (per police committees)). Provision for amalgamation of town with county forces		
General Police and Improvement (Scotland) Act 1862	1850 powers extended to any area with population over 700		
Public Health (Scotland) Act 1867		Duties and powers to town councils and police commissioners. Outwith towns, powers to parochial boards	Special districts set up for supply to villages, etc.
1889–1929	County councils take over police of any burgh with population less than 7000 – under standing joint committee of county councillors and commissioners of supply		Parochial board powers transferred to county councils (or per district committees)
Burgh Police (Scotland) Act 1892	Consolidated and extended existing legislation; In future, only burghs with population over 20,000 able to establish police forces		

Legislation	Police	Lighting/paving scavenging	Water supply/ sewage
Local Government (Scotland) Act 1894		Special districts permitted, per county councils or district committees	
Public Health (Scotland) Act 1897		Extended powers and duties of responsible bodies (county councils, district committees, town councils, police commissioners)	
Town Councils (Scotland) Act 1900	Police commissioners and police burghs abolished. Uniform type of burgh established with powers vested in a town council		
Burgh Police (Scotland) Act 1903	Detailed amendments and extensions to 1892 Act		
1929–74	Minimum population for police authority set at 50,000. Authorities with existing forces and population over 20,000 allowed to retain them. All others transferred to county councils	Powers retained by existing authorities	Many ad hoc boards and trusts gradually established through combination of different local authorities
Water (Scotland) Act 1949			Special districts abolished
Police (Scotland) Act 1956	Provided for amalgamation of police authorities (only 20 by 1969)		
Water (Scotland) Act 1967			Water boards established (ad hoc bodies with members drawn from county councils)
1975–	All powers to regional councils (some joint)	All powers to district councils	Water boards under aegis of regional councils

Social Services

Legislation	Social Welfare/Poor relief	Hospitals/Health
1832–89	Administered by joint boards of kirk sessions and heritors; town councils in burghs	Hospitals mainly charitable foundations, sometimes supported by town councils
Poor Law (Scotland) Amendment Act 1845	Establishment of parochial boards to administer poor relief and poor houses	Powers to parochial boards in county areas to give financial aid to hospitals
Lunacy (Scotland) Act 1857		Established district lunacy boards and lunatic asylums
Public Health (Scotland) Act 1867		Powers to town councils, police commissioners and parochial boards to erect hospitals. Also powers to combat disease and to regulate lodging houses
1889–1929 Burgh Police (Scotland) Act 1892		County council medical officers of health appointed, took over most functions of parochial boards Town Councils obliged to appoint medical officers of health and sanitary inspectors
Local Government (Scotland) Act 1894	Parochial boards replaced by parish councils	
Public Health (Scotland) Act 1897		Further powers to county councils, district committees, town councils and police commissioners
Old Age Pensions Act 1908	Began process of state control of social welfare	
National Insurance Act 1911	Introduced unemployment insurance	
Mental Deficiency and Lunacy (Scotland) Act 1913		District boards of control replaced lunacy boards – administered by county councils and town councils

Legislation	Social Welfare/Poor relief	Hospitals/Health
1929–74	Parish councils abolished. Powers transferred to county councils (or per district councils) and large burghs	Responsibility retained by county councils (district councils) and large burghs. Small burghs with restricted powers. Large burghs and county councils took over district boards of control
Unemployment Act 1934	Transferred relief for chronic unemployed to state Unemployment Assistance Board	
National Health Service (Scotland) Act 1947		Curative health services taken over by state. Preventive health remained with county councils and large burghs
National Assistance Act 1948	Welfare payments became state responsibility. Welfare services remained with county councils and large burghs	
Social Work (Scotland) Act 1968	Brought together functions of health, welfare and care of children	
1975–	All social work and health functions transferred to regional councils	

Housing/Planning	Roads	Education
1832–89	Town councils responsible for urban roads by common law. In counties, roads maintained by statute labour or through turnpike trusts, administered by road trustees. Turnpike acts consolidated in Turnpike Acts of 1823 and 1831 1845 General Statute Labour Act – ended statute labour	Parish schools the responsibility of kirk session and heritors. Town councils responsible for burgh schools

Housing/Planning	Roads	Education
		Education (Scotland) Act 1872 – all powers transferred to school boards
	Roads and Bridges (Scotland) Act 1878 – turnpikes phased out and roads to be responsibility of county road trustees in rural areas and town councils and police commissioners in burghs	
1889–1929 Housing of the Working Class Act 1890 – powers to town councils, police commissioners and county councils for slum clearance, improvement and council house building	County councils took over from county road trustees	
Housing, Town Planning, etc. (Scotland) Act 1909 – imposed duties on town councils and county councils to submit proposals for housing development Housing (Scotland) Act 1925 – consolidated legislation	Roads Act 1920 – gave Ministry of Transport powers to build and maintain roads	Education (Scotland) Act 1908 – County education committees to administer grants for secondary education Education (Scotland) Act 1918 – school boards replaced by education authorities

Education (Scotland) Act 1928 – education authorities replaced by county councils (per education committees) |

Housing/Planning	Roads	Education
1929–74	County councils took over control of artery roads in small burghs	County councils remain sole authorities
Powers retained by county councils and all town councils		
Housing (Scotland) Act 1930 – further powers for clearance and demolition	Trunk Roads Act 1936 and Trunk Roads Act 1946 transferred trunk roads to Ministry of Transport and subsequently to Secretary of State for Scotland	
Town and Country Planning Act 1932 – county councils and large town councils to pursue plans for 'betterment'		
Housing (Scotland) Act 1935 – powers to rehouse overcrowded areas		
Town and Country Planning (Scotland) Act 1947 – made development plans compulsory (large town councils and county councils)		
Housing (Scotland) Act 1950 – consolidated prevous acts – removed clauses referring to 'working class'		
1975–	Local authority powers transferred to regional councils	Powers transferred to regional councils
Most powers transferred to district councils		

FURTHER READING AND INFORMATION

Chapter 1. Introduction, pages 8–13

KIRKLAND, HILARY, 'Developments in Scottish local history', *University of Edinburgh Journal*, volume 30, no. 4, December 1982, pp. 294–6.

ROGERS, ALAN, *Approaches to Local History*, 2nd edition, Longman, 1977.

The Scottish Local History Forum, which publishes a magazine *Scottish Local History*, aims to bring together all those with an interest, amateur or professional, in Scottish local history.

Scotland's Cultural Heritage is a project administered by the University of Edinburgh, with premises at the History of Medicine and Science Unit, High School Yards, Drummond Street, Edinburgh EH1 1LZ. It can provide assistance with publishing, graphic services and exhibitions.

Major societies for the study of aspects of Scottish history include:

The Scottish History Society (which publishes edited volumes of source materials)

The Scottish Record Society (which publishes transcriptions from Scottish records)

The Scottish Economic and Social History Society (which publishes a journal of contributed articles)

The Company of Scottish History (which publishes the *Scottish History Review*)

Three English-based magazines are:

Exploring Local History (published by Elmscrest publishing)

The Local Historian (published by the National Council of Social Service for the Standing Conference for Local History)

Local History (available from Local History, Freepost, Nottingham, NG7 1BR)

The Consultative Committee on the Curriculum publishes a newsletter, *Scottish Resources in School Projects*.

Chapter 2. The Public Library and its collections, pages 14–32

Bibliographies

In addition to the major bibliographies mentioned in the text, the following are worth consulting:

Bibliotheca Scotica: a catalogue of books relating to Scotland, Smith, 1926.

BLACK, GEORGE F., *A List of Works Relating to Scotland*, New York Public Library, 1916.

GRANT, ERIC, *Scotland*, Clio Press, 1982.

Scottish Material Culture: a Bibliography, National Museum of Antiquities of Scotland (irregular).

Local history libraries

Information about library authorities and record offices and their collections is given in:
ARMSTRONG, NORMA E. S., *Local Collections in Scotland*, SLA, 1977.
MCADAMS, FRANK, and TAIT, HEATHER, *Scottish Library and Information Resources, 1984–85*, SLA, 1984 (this work is updated periodically).
The Scottish Group of the Local Studies Group of the Library Association publishes the journal *Locscot*.

Newspapers

COWAN, R. M. W., *The Newspaper in Scotland: a Study of its First Expansion 1815–60*, Outram, 1946.
ELLIOTT, B. J., 'A Scottish local newspaper as a source of local history', *Forth Naturalist and Historian*, vol. III, 1978, pp. 128–32.

Topographical prints

HOLLOWAY, M., *A Bibliography of Nineteenth Century British Topographical Books with Steel Engravings*, Holland Press, 1977.
RUSSELL, RONALD, *Guide to British Topographical Prints*, David & Charles, 1979.
Popular collections of Scottish topographical prints include:
BEATTIE, W., *Scotland Illustrated in a Series of Views*, Virtue, 1838 (119 steel engravings; later extended and published under the title *Caledonia Illustrated*).
DANIELL, W. and AYTON, R., *A Voyage round Great Britain*, Longman, 1814–25 (contains 156 Scottish coastal scenes).
FORSYTH, R., *The Beauties of Scotland*, Constable etc., 1805–8 (over 100 copper engraved plates).
GARNETT, T., *Observations on a Tour through the Highlands and Part of the Western Isles of Scotland*, Stockdale, 1800 (51 tinted aquatints).
LAWSON, JOHN PARKER, *Scotland Delineated*, Day & Son, 1847–54 (71 tinted lithographs).

Photographs

HANNAVY, J., *A Moment in Time: Scottish Contributions to Photography 1840–1920*, Third Eye Centre, 1983.
A directory of photographic holdings of all libraries and other institutions is:
Picture Sources UK, Macdonald: Society of Picture Researchers and Editors, 1985.

Postcards

BYATT, ANTHONY, *Picture Postcards and their Publishers*, Golden Age Postcard Books, 1978.
CARLINE, R., *Pictures in the Post: the Story of the Picture Postcard*, Gordon Fraser, 1971.
DUVAL, WILLIAM and MONAHAN, VALERIE, *Collecting Postcards in Colour 1894–1914*, Blandford Press, 1978.
MONAHAN, VALERIE, *Collecting Postcards in Colour 1914–1930*, Blandford Press, 1980.

Stanley Gibbons Postcard Catalogue, 4th edition, Gibbons, 1984.

Ephemera

LEWIS, JOHN, *Collecting Printed Ephemera*, Studio Vista, 1976.
RICKARDS, MAURICE, *Posters at the Turn of the Century*, Evelyn, Adams and Mackay, 1968.
RICKARDS, MAURICE, *Posters: the 1920s*, Evelyn, Adams and Mackay, 1968.
RICKARDS, MAURICE, *The Public Notice: an Illustrative History*, David and Charles, 1973.
WOOD, ROBERT, *Children 1773–1840*, Evans, 1969 (History at Source Series).
WOOD, ROBERT, *Entertainments 1800–1900*, Evans, 1970 (History at Source Series).
WOOD, ROBERT, *Law and Order 1725–1886*, Evans, 1971 (History at Source Series).

Collecting

MACKAY, JAMES, *Collecting Local History*, Longman, 1984.
A list of antiquarian booksellers in Scotland appears in:
Scottish Book Browsers Guide, Gruther Publications, 1985.

Chapter 3. Archive Offices and their Records, pages 33–66

Archive offices

CENTRAL REGION., *Inventory of Central Region Archives Department*, Central Region, 1977.
DELL, RICHARD F., 'Local archive service in Scotland since reorganisation', *Journal of the Society of Archivists*, vol. v, no. 6, October 1976, pp. 357–68.
IREDALE, DAVID, 'Moray District Record Office', *SLA News*, November–December 1979, pp. 414–18.
RODGER, R. G., 'Scottish archives and local government reorganisation', *Local Historian*, vol. xiv, no. 2, May 1980, pp. 98–100.
SLA News, no. 186, March–April 1985 (various relevant articles in this issue).

Archive Offices established by 1985

Note: regions inherited county council and districts inherited town council archives, though local co-operative arrangements vary (some records, scandalously, are virtually inaccessible). Older burgh records, especially deeds and sasines, are held by the Scottish Record Office.

BORDERS REGION
Borders Regional Library Headquarters, St Mary's Mill, Selkirk TD7 5EW holds county council archives, but no records have as yet been devolved from the Scottish Record Office. Town council records are retained by respective burghs.

CENTRAL REGION
Central Regional Archives, Old High School, Spittal Street, Stirling FK8 1DG.

DUMFRIES AND GALLOWAY REGION
The Ewart Library, Catherine Street, Dumfries DG1 1JB holds county council archives. Town council records are held by district councils.

FIFE REGION
Fife records are dispersed among various repositories: St Andrews University Archives, Dunfermline Library, Kirkcaldy Town House, Kirkcaldy Museum, the Educational Resource Centre in Kirkcaldy and Fife House, Glenrothes.

GRAMPIAN REGION
Grampian Regional Council Archives, Department of Law and Administration, Woodhill House, Ashgrove Road West, Aberdeen AB9 2LA.
There are also two district archives:
Aberdeen District Archives, Town House, Aberdeen AB9 1AQ.
Moray District Record Office, The Tollbooth, High Street, Forres, IV36 0AB.

HIGHLAND REGION
Highland Region Reference and Archive Services, Farraline Park, Inverness IV1 1NH (limited opening – no records transferred from Scottish Record Office).

LOTHIAN REGION
Midlothian county and East Lothian records are held in the Scottish Record Office, West Lothian records by West Lothian District Library, Midlothian school log books by Midlothian District Library and Edinburgh city records and those of Midlothian burghs by:
Edinburgh City Archives, City Chambers, Edinburgh EH1 1PL.

ORKNEY
Orkney Library, Archives Department, Laing Street, Kirkwall, Orkney KW15 1NW.

SHETLAND
Shetland Library, Lower Hillhead, Lerwick, Shetland ZE1 0EL.

STRATHCLYDE REGION
Strathclyde Regional Archives, Mitchell Library, North Street, Glasgow G3 7DN.
There are also two branches, for Argyllshire and Ayrshire records respectively. Argyll and Bute District, Court House, Inveraray.
County Buildings, Wellington Square, Ayr.
Several district libraries hold district archives.

TAYSIDE REGION
Dundee City District Archive and Record Centre, 14 City Square, Dundee has overall responsibility for all Tayside records. A District Archive for Perth and Kinross forms part of the Perth Town library:
The Sandeman Library, Kinnoull Street, Perth.

WESTERN ISLES
No records have been transferred. Isle of Lewis District Council holds Stornoway town records.

Using archives
EMMISON, F. G., *How to Read Local Archives 1550–1700*, Historical
Association, 1967.
GOODER, EILEEN A., *Latin for Local History: an Introduction*, 2nd edition,
Longman, 1978.
LATHAM, R. E., *Revised Medieval Latin Word List*, Oxford University
Press, 1965.
SIMPSON, GRANT G., *Scottish Handwriting 1150–1560*, Bratton, 1973.
The Scottish Records Association, set up in 1977, is concerned with the
preservation and use of public and private records.

Scottish Record Office

The following leaflets are available free of charge:
A Short Guide to the Records
The Register House Plans Collection
History of the National Archives
Facilities for Historical Research
Facilities for Local History Groups
Using our Archives
Search Room Information: Historical and West Search Rooms
The Scottish Record Office
Sources for Family History
The Scottish Record Office also circulates a free newsletter. The annual
reports include lists of new accessions and often feature different parts of
the collection. An important article is:
SANDERSON, M. H. B., 'Sources for Scottish local history – the Scottish
Record Office', *Local Historian*, vol. XI, 1974, pp. 123–9.

Historical background: Scottish history

The researcher has the choice of three multi-volume histories of Scotland.
The oldest, two-volume set is:
DICKINSON, WILLIAM CROFT, *Scotland from Earliest Times to 1603*, 3rd
edition, Oxford University Press, 1977.
PRYDE, GEORGE S., *Scotland from 1603 to the Present Day*, Nelson, 1962.
The standard modern history, with substantial bibliographies of primary
and secondary sources, is the four-volume work *Edinburgh History of
Scotland*. Of the three series, it contains the least information about local
affairs.
DUNCAN, A. A. M., *The Making of the Kingdom*, Oliver & Boyd, 1975.
NICHOLSON, RANALD, *The Later Middle Ages*, Oliver & Boyd, 1974.
DONALDSON, GORDON, *James V–James VII*, Oliver & Boyd, 1965.
FERGUSON, WILLIAM, *1689 to the Present*, Oliver & Boyd, 1968.
The most recent series is the *New History of Scotland*, published in eight
volumes by Edward Arnold. Some of the volumes have a great deal on
social and economic issues, though local institutions are not always
investigated in depth:
SMYTH, ALFRED P., *War Lords and Holy Men: Scotland 500–1000*, Arnold,
1983.
BARROW, G. W. S., *Kingship and Unity: Scotland 1000–1306*, Arnold,
1981.
GRANT, ALEXANDER, *Independence and Nationhood: Scotland 1306–1469*,
Arnold, 1984.

WORMALD, JENNY, *Court, Kirk and Community: Scotland 1470–1625*, Arnold, 1981.
MITCHISON, ROSALIND, *Lordship to Patronage: Scotland 1603–1745*, Arnold, 1983.
LENMAN, BRUCE, *Integration, Enlightenment and Industrialization: Scotland 1746–1832*, Arnold, 1981.
CHECKLAND, SYDNEY and CHECKLAND, OLIVE, *Industry and Ethos: Scotland 1832–1914*, Arnold, 1984.
HARVIE, CHRISTOPHER, *No Gods and Precious Few Heroes: Scotland 1914–1980*, Arnold, 1981.

Historical background: Church history

A bibliographical guide, now considerably out of date but useful for older material is:
MACGREGOR, MALCOLM B., *Sources and Literature of Scottish Church History*, McCallum, 1934.
Church of Scotland records are described in:
Records of the Church of Scotland Preserved in the Scottish Record Office and General Register Office, Scottish Record Society, 1967.
The Scottish Church History Society encourages and advises on the study of Church history.
The following volumes of Scottish supplications to Rome have been published by the Scottish History Society:
Calendar of Scottish Supplications to Rome 1418–1422, 1934.
Calendar of Scottish Supplications to Rome 1423–1428, 1956.
Calendar of Scottish Supplications to Rome 1428–1432, 1970.
and by the University of Glasgow:
Calendar of Scottish Supplications to Rome 1433–1447, 1983.

Historical background: local government

A general study of the history of local administration is still wanting. Of the literature available, the most useful is probably:
McLARTY, M. R., *Source Book and History of Administrative Law in Scotland*, Hodge, 1956.
Also to be consulted are:
SHAW, JAMES E., *Local Government in Scotland, Past, Present and Future*, Oliver & Boyd, 1942.
SKINNER, B. C., 'Local history of Scotland', *Scottish Historical Review*, vol. XLVII, no. 2, October 1968, pp. 160–7.
Local administration is also dealt with at length in:
WALKER, DAVID M., *The Scottish Legal System*, 5th edition, W. Green, 1981. This work is also a particularly valuable guide to all legal sources and the development of Scots law.
Of early forms of local administration, the best studied are those of the burghs:
MACKENZIE, WILLIAM MCKAY, *The Scottish Burghs*, Oliver & Boyd, 1949.
MURRAY, DAVID, *Early Burgh Organisation in Scotland*, Jackson Wylie, 1932 (2 vols).
The researcher will also find much of value in the publications of the Scottish Burgh Records Society. There is also some bibliographical coverage in this field:

MARTIN, GEOFFREY HOWARD and MCINTYRE, SYLVIA, *A Bibliography of British and Irish Municipal History*, Leicester University Press, 1972, vol. I, pp. 581–640.

Barony courts and early sheriff courts are discussed respectively in the introductions to the following, both written by William Croft Dickinson:

The Court Book of the Barony of Carnwath 1523–1542, Scottish History Society, 1937.

The Sheriff Court Book of Fife 1515–1522, Scottish History Society, 1928.

One area which has been the subject of a rigorous historical study is eighteenth-century county government. It is valuable background reading for anyone interested in the records of rural areas before the advent of county councils:

WHETSTONE, ANN E., *Scottish County Government in the Eighteenth and Nineteenth Centuries*, John Donald, 1981.

Detailed study of local government since 1832 is possible only through the use of textbooks of administrative law written for contemporary use:

GOUDY, H. and SMITH, W. C., *Local Government in Scotland*, Blackwood, 1880.

MURRAY, A., *Councillor's Manual: Being a Guide to Scottish Local Government*, W. Green, 1892. This work was reprinted in 13 different editions up to 1933; it consists of extracts from current statutes, and the different editions can be used to trace changes in local government functions. The same applies to:

WHYTE, W. E., *Local Government in Scotland*, Hodge, 1925 (with a second edition in 1936 after the far-reaching changes brought about in the Local Government (Scotland) Act, 1929).

The period from 1929 up to local government reorganisation in 1973 can be investigated through:

MILLER, J. BENNETT, *An Outline of Administrative and Local Government Law in Scotland*, W. Green, 1961 (2nd edition 1964).

Scots law and legal records

ANTONIO, DAVID G., *Scots Law for Administrative, Commercial and Professional Students*, Collins, 1968 (a layman's introduction).

BEATON, J. A., *Scots Legal Terms and Expressions*, W. Green, 1982.

GLOAG, W. M. and HENDERSON, R. C., *Introduction to the Law of Scotland*, 8th edition, W. Green, 1980.

An Introduction to Scottish Legal History, Stair Society, 1958.

An Introductory Survey of the Sources and Literature of Scots Law, Stair Society, 1936.

MARSHALL, ENID A., *General Principles of Scots Law*, 4th edition, W. Green, 1982.

WALKER, DAVID M., *Principles of Scottish Private Law*, 3rd edition, Oxford University Press, 1983 (4 volumes).

A very useful bibliography of all aspects of Scots law, past and present, is:

MAXWELL, LESLIE F. and MAXWELL, W. HAROLD, *Scottish Law to 1956*, vol. v of *A Legal Bibliography of the British Commonwealth of Nations*, 2nd edition, Sweet & Maxwell, 1957.

Two important societies in the area are the publishing Stair Society and the Scottish Legal History Group.

Public and private records

The two main studies of public records with national significance are:
PATON, H. M., *The Scottish Records: Their History and Value*, Historical Association of Scotland, 1933.
THOMSON, J. M., *The Public Records of Scotland*, Maclenox Jackson, 1922.
Also worth consulting is:
FERGUSSON, JAMES, 'The public records of Scotland', *Archives*, no. 8, 1953, pp. 30–8; no. 9, 1953, pp. 4–10.
The best introduction to pre-Reformation law, local institutions and records is:
INNES, COSMO, *Scotch Legal Antiquities*, Edmonston & Douglas, 1872.
There is no large-scale study of Scottish local records. Those with a legal slant are, however, covered in:
An Introductory Survey of the Sources and Literature of Scots Law, Stair Society, 1936.
Also to be consulted is:
IMRIE, JOHN and SIMPSON, GRANT G., 'Local archives of Great Britain. XV. Local and private archives of Scotland', *Archives*, vol. 3, no. 19, 1958, pp. 135–47, 219–30.
Private archives are discussed in:
DONALDSON, WILLIAM, 'Reports and surveys of archives in northern Scotland', *Northern Scotland*, vol. 3, no. 2, 1979–80, pp. 159–72.
TOUGH, ALISTAIR and JOHNSTON, DOROTHY B., 'Reports and surveys of archives in northern Scotland', *Northern Scotland*, vol. 4, nos. 1–2, 1981, pp. 121–38.
Inventories and surveys of private archives carried out by the Royal Commission on Historical Manuscripts are listed in the bibliography:
Publications of the Royal Commission on Historical Manuscripts, HMSO, irregular (Government Publications Sectional List 17).

Parliamentary papers

LAMBERT, S., *List of House of Commons Sessional Papers 1701–50*, Swift, 1968.
LAMBERT, S., *House of Commons Sessional Papers of the 18th Century*, vol. I, *Introduction and List 1715–60*; vol. II, *List 1761–1800*, Scholarly Resources, 1975/6.
FORD, PERCY and FORD, GRACE, *Select List of British Parliamentary Papers 1833–1899*, Blackwell, 1953.
FORD, PERCY and FORD, GRACE, *Select List of British Parliamentary Papers 1900–1954*, Blackwell, 1951–61 (3 volumes).
FORD, PERCY, *Select List of British Parliamentary Papers 1955–1964*, Irish University Press, 1970.
MARSHALLSAY, DIANA and SMITH, J. H., *Ford List of British Parliamentary Papers, 1965–1974*, KTO Press, 1979.
GREAT BRITAIN. Parliament. House of Commons, *General Index to the Bills, Reports, Estimates, Accounts and Papers Printed by Order of the House of Commons*, HMSO, 1870–1960 (in seven volumes covering the years 1801–1949).

Chapter 4. The Individual and the Community, pages 67–87

Family history

Three recent general guides are as follows:

HAMILTON-EDWARDS, GERALD, *In Search of Scottish Ancestry*, 2nd edition, Phillimore, 1983.

JAMES, ALWYN, *Scottish Roots*, MacDonald (Midlothian), 1981 (concentrates on a detailed examination of the records in the General Register Office).

WHYTE, DONALD, *Introducing Scottish Genealogical Research*, 3rd edition, Scottish Genealogy Society, 1982.

The soundest short exposition is still the introduction to:

STUART, MARGARET, *Guide to Works of Reference on the History and Genealogy of Scottish Families*, Oliver & Boyd, 1930 (facsimile reprint by Genealogical Publishing Company, 1979).

Sources for family history are listed in:

STEEL, DONALD JOHN, *Sources for Scottish Genealogy and Family History*, vol. XII of the *National Index of Parish Registers*, Society of Genealogists, 1970.

Emigration is a subject of great interest to many living in North America and the Commonwealth. There is a large literature, and two bibliographies:

HIGHLAND REGIONAL COUNCIL. *Library Service, Emigration from the Highlands 1800–1900*, The Library Service, 1979.

WHYTE, DONALD, 'Scottish Emigration: a Select Bibliography', *Scottish Genealogist*, vol. XXI, 1974, pp. 65–86.

Registers of emigrants from ship passenger lists and associated sources include:

DOBSON, DAVID, *Directory of Scottish Settlers in North America 1625–1825*, vol. I, Genealogical Publishing Company, 1984.

TEPPER, MICHAEL, *New World Immigrants: a Consolidation of Ship Passenger Lists and Associated Data from Periodical Literature*, Genealogical Publishing Company, 1979 (2 volumes).

The exploitation of family photographs and mementoes is the subject of:

STEEL, DON and TAYLOR, LAURENCE, *Family History in Focus*, Lutterworth, 1984.

Pre-1855 parish registers are listed in:

REGISTRAR-GENERAL FOR SCOTLAND, *Detailed List of the Old Parochial Registers of Scotland*, HMSO, 1872.

Published family histories are listed in:

FERGUSON, JOAN, *Scottish Family Histories Held in Scottish Libraries*, Scottish Central Library, 1960 (new edition pending from the National Library of Scotland).

There are two important societies:

Scots Ancestry Research Society, 3 Albany Street, Edinburgh EH1 3PY.

Scottish Genealogy Society, 9, Union Street, Edinburgh EH1 3LT.

The latter publishes the *Scottish Genealogist*, a journal full of practical information about the use of Scottish records.

The Family Tree Magazine is published from 129 Great Whyte, Ramsey, Huntingdon, Cambs, PE17 1HP.

Gravestones

JONES, JEREMY, *How to Record Gravestones*, 2nd edition, Council for British

Archaeology, 1979.
WHITE, H. LESLIE, *Monuments and Their Inscriptions: a Practical Guide*,
Society of Genealogists, 1978.
Architectural styles are the subject of:
WILLSHER, BETTY and HUNTER, DOREEN, *Stones: a Guide to Some
Remarkable Eighteenth Century Gravestones*, Canongate, 1978.
WILLSHER, BETTY, *Scottish Graveyards*, Chambers, 1985.
For the latter subject, consult also the indexes to the *Proceedings of the
Society of Antiquaries Scotland.*

Oral recording

HENEGE, DAVID, *Oral Historiography*, Longman, 1982.
HOWARTH, KEN, *An Introduction to Sound Recording for the Oral Historian
and the Sound Archivist*, North West Sound Archive, 1977.
HUMPHRIES, STEPHEN, *Handbook of Oral History*, Inter-Action Imprint,
1984.
THOMPSON, PAUL, *The Voice of the Past: Oral History*, Oxford University
Press, 1978.
The Scottish Oral History Group publishes a newsletter and arranges
classes on aspects of oral history and recording.
The Oral History Society publishes the journal *Oral History.*

Labour history

A bibliography now somewhat out of date is:
MACDOUGALL, IAN, *An Interim Bibliography of the Scottish Working Class
Movement and of Other Labour Records Held in Scotland*, Society for the
Study of Labour History: Scottish Committee, 1965.
Source materials are the subject of:
MACDOUGALL, IAN, *A Catalogue of Some Labour Records in Scotland and
Some Scots Records Outside Scotland*, Scottish Labour History Society,
1978.
Labour history is the subject of the following works:
MACDOUGALL, IAN, *Essays in Scottish Labour History*, John Donald, 1978.
MACDOUGALL, IAN, *Labour in Scotland*, Mainstream, 1984.

Schooling

There is good bibliographical coverage in this area:
CRAIGIE, JAMES, *A Bibliography of Scottish Education Before 1872*,
University of London Press, 1970.
CRAIGIE, JAMES, *A Bibliography of Scottish Education 1872–1972*, University
of London Press, 1974.
There is also an extensive bibliography in:
SCOTLAND, JAMES, *History of Scottish Education*, University of London
Press, 1969 (2 volumes).
For burgh schools, the standard text is still:
GRANT, JAMES, *History of the Burgh Schools in Scotland*, Collins, 1876.
The Scottish Council for Research in Education, 15 St John Street,
Edinburgh EH8 8JR has published a variety of historical studies in
education, including local studies.
The Scottish Record Office has produced a source list for schools.

Social welfare

FERGUSON, THOMAS, *The Dawn of Scottish Social Welfare*, Nelson, 1948.
FERGUSON, THOMAS, *Scottish Social Welfare 1864–1914*, E. & S. Livingstone, 1958.
Poor Law and poor relief are the subject of:
CAGE, R. A., *Scottish Poor Law 1745–1845*, Scottish Academic Press, 1981.
CORMACK, ALEX A., *Poor Relief in Scotland: An Outline of the Growth and Administration of the Poor Laws in Scotland from the Middle Ages to the Present Day*, D. Wyllie & Son, 1923.
Hospital and health services are studied in:
BROTHERSTON, J. H. T., *Observations on the Early Public Health Movement in Scotland*, H. K. Lewis, 1952.
COMRIE, J. D., *History of Scottish Medicine to 1860*, 2nd edition, Baillière, 1932 (2 volumes).
HAMILTON, D., *The Healers: A History of Scottish Medicine*, Canongate, 1981.
Hospitals records are discussed in:
WALTON, P. M. EAVES, 'Hospital archives', *Scottish Genealogist*, vol. xxv, no. 3, September 1978, pp. 65–72.
A Newsletter is published by the Scottish Society of the History of Medicine. An annual bibliography of contributions to Scottish social history is included in the journal *Scottish Economic and Social History*.

Chapter 5. Buildings Past and Present, pages 88–106

Archaeology

As well as the bibliographies and sources mentioned in the text, the following can be consulted:
Scottish Material Culture: A Bibliography: Section A: Archaeology, National Museum of Antiquities (irregular).
The methodology of archaeology is studied in:
BARKER, PHILIP, *Techniques of Archaeological Excavation*, Batsford, 1977.
CLARKE, DAVID L., *Analytical Archaeology*, 2nd edition, Methuen, 1978.
CLARKE, DAVID L., *Models in Archaeology*, Methuen, 1972.
Simple guides to interpreting archaeological data have been published by the Council for British Archaeology:
CORBISHLEY, MIKE, *Archaeology in the Town*, Council for British Archaeology, 1982.
CROFT, ROBERT, *Archaeology and Science*, Council for British Archaeology, 1982.
STEANE, JOHN, *Archaeology in the Countryside*, Council for British Archaeology, 1982.
Prehistoric Scotland is the subject of a series of books in the *Regional Archaeology Series* published by Heinemann. Three general guides are:
FEACHEM, R., *Guide to Prehistoric Scotland*, Batsford, 1963.
MACKIE, E. W., *Scotland: An Archaeological Guide*, Faber, 1975.
RITCHIE, GRAHAM and ANNA, *Scotland: Archaeology and Early History*, Thames & Hudson, 1981.

Recording buildings

The general guide by Brunskill (1978) mentioned in the text unfortunately is applicable in detail only to English features. The nearest equivalents for Scotland are studies of rural architecture listed in the section on architecture.

ADDYMAN, P. and MORRIS, M. K., *The Archaeological Study of Churches*, Council for British Archaeology, 1976.

BUCHANAN, TERRY, *Photographing Historic Buildings for the Record*, Royal Commission on Historical Monuments, 1984.

COCKE, THOMAS, *Recording a Church: An Illustrated Glossary*, 2nd edition, Council for British Archaeology, 1984.

The Scottish Vernacular Buildings Working Group publishes a newsletter and organizes practical sessions on conducting building surveys.

Industrial archaeology is the subject of:

BUTT, JOHN, *Industrial Archaeology of Scotland*, David & Charles, 1967.

HUME, JOHN R., *Industrial Archaeology of Scotland*, vol. I, *The Lowlands and Borders*, Batsford, 1976; vol. II, *The Highlands and Islands*, Batsford, 1977.

MAJOR, J. K., *Fieldwork in Industrial Archaeology*, Batsford, 1975.

The Scottish Industrial Heritage Society publishes a newsletter and organizes courses on industrial archaeology. The Scottish Industrial Archaeology Survey Unit is attached to the Royal Commission on the Ancient and Historical Monuments of Scotland.

Houses and housing

The study of property registers will be helped by the use of:

CRAIGIE, JOHN, *Scottish Law of Conveyancing: Moveable Rights*, 2nd edition, Bell & Bradfute, 1894.

CRAIGIE, JOHN, *Scottish Law of Conveyancing: Heritable Rights*, 3rd edition, Bell & Bradfute, 1899.

The social history of housing is the subject of:

GAULDIE, ENID, *Cruel Habitations: A History of Working Class Housing 1780–1918*, Allen & Unwin 1974 (a study based on Glasgow).

NIVEN, DOUGLAS, *The Development of Housing in Scotland*, Croom Helm, 1979.

An example of a study of Scottish upper-class household life is:

MARSHALL, ROSALIND K., *The Days of Duchess Anne; Life in the Household of the Duchess of Hamilton 1656–1716*, Collins, 1973.

The *Review of Scottish Culture* is a new journal covering the applied and decorative arts and all aspects of the life and work of the people, with essays on 'ships, wooden locks, sheilings, tenements, claypipes, box-beds and bannocks'.

Architecture

A guide to relevant archives is:

DUNBAR, JOHN G., 'Source materials for the study of Scottish architectural history', *Art Libraries Historian*, vol. IV, no. 3, Autumn 1979, pp. 17–26.

A general bibliography is by:

HALL, R. DE ZOUCHE, *A Bibliography on Vernacular Architecture*, David & Charles, 1972.

The development of Scottish building styles is followed in:

DUNBAR, JOHN G., *The Architecture of Scotland*, 2nd edition, Batsford, 1978.
Rural architecture is the theme of:
FENTON, ALEXANDER and WALKER, BRUCE, *The Rural Architecture of Scotland*, John Donald, 1981.
NAISMITH, ROBERT J., *Buildings of the Scottish Countryside*, Gollancz, 1985.
Early church buildings can be studied in:
FAWCETT, RICHARD, *Scottish Medieval Churches*, Scottish Development Department: Historic Buildings and Monuments Directorate, 1985.
Drawings of architectural features make up:
Details of Scottish Architecture, Edinburgh Architectural Association, 1922.
Examples of Scottish Architecture from the Twelfth to the Seventeenth Century, Board of Trustees for the National Galleries of Scotland, 1921–33 (4 volumes).

Chapter 6. Settlement Studies: History of a Village, Town or Parish, pages 107–37

Historical geography

There is a recent guide to sources:
WHYTE, IAN and WHYTE, K. A., *Sources for Scottish Historical Geography*, Geo Abstracts, 1981.
Models and methodology are discussed in:
CARTER, HAROLD, *An Introduction to Urban Historical Geography*, Arnold, 1983.
CARTER, HAROLD, *The Study of Urban Geography*, 3rd edition, Arnold, 1981.
JONES, EMRYS and EYLES, JOHN, *An Introduction to Social Geography*, Oxford University Press, 1971.
Studies in Scottish historical geography include:
ADAMS, IAN H., *The Making of Urban Scotland*, Croom Helm, 1978.
CLAPPERTON, CHALMERS M., *Scotland: a New Study*, David & Charles, 1983.
MILLMAN, R. N., *The Making of the Scottish Landscape*, Batsford, 1975.
PARRY, M. L. and SLATER, T. R., *The Making of the Scottish Countryside*, Croom Helm, 1980.
TURNOCK, DAVID, *The Historical Geography of Scotland since 1707*, Cambridge University Press, 1982.
WHITTINGTON, G. and WHYTE, I. D., *An Historical Geography of Scotland*, Academic Press, 1983.
The December issue of the *Scottish Geographical Magazine* contains a survey of the previous year's literature on Scottish geography.

Maps and plans

Use of materials is discussed in:
DICKINSON, G. C., *Maps and Air Photographs*, 2nd edition, Arnold, 1979.
PARRY, MARTIN L., 'County maps as historical sources: a sequence of surveys of South East Scotland', *Scottish Studies*, vol. XIX, 1975, pp. 15–26.
ST JOSEPH, J. K., *The Uses of Air Photography*, 2nd edition, John Baker, 1977.

A bibliographical guide to Scottish cartography is:
MOORE, JOHN N., *The Mapping of Scotland: A Guide to the Literature of Scottish Cartography Prior to the Ordnance Survey*, University of Aberdeen: Department of Geography (1983?).
Modern reconstructions of the Scottish landscape make up:
MCNEILL, PETER and NICHOLSON, RANALD, *An Historical Atlas of Scotland c400–c1600*, Atlas Committee of the Conference of Scottish Medievalists, 1976.

Communications

Roads are studied in:
FENTON, ALEXANDER and STEEL, GEOFFREY, *Loads and Roads in Scotland and Beyond*, John Donald, 1984.
TAYLOR, WILLIAM, *The Military Roads in Scotland*, David & Charles, 1976.
A monograph on the canals of Scotland is:
LINDSAY, JEAN, *The Canals of Scotland*, David & Charles, 1968.
There is a large literature on railways in Scotland. Most of the private companies are the subjects of a series of books published by David & Charles, who have also produced regional guides to the railway network (6 volumes).
Early railways are the subject of:
ROBERTSON, C. J. A., *The Origins of the Scottish Railway System 1722–1844*, John Donald, 1983.
Source guides include the following:
ANDERSON-SMITH, MYRTLE, 'The O'Dell Railway Collection in Aberdeen University Library', *LocScot*, vol. I, no. 8, Spring 1985, pp. 150–3.
OTTLEY, GEORGE, *Railway History: A Guide to 61 Collections in Libraries and Archives in Great Britain*, Library Association, 1972.

Place names

JOHNSTON, JAMES B., *Place Names of Scotland*, S. R. Publishers, 1970 (reprint of the 3rd edition of 1934).
WALTER, GEORGE, *Bibliography of the Place Names of Scotland*, Royal Scottish Geographical Society, 1945 (typescript).

Landownership

SHAW, SAMUEL, *An Accurate Alphabetical Index of the Registered Entails in Scotland 1685–1784*, Shaw, 1784.

Agriculture

Three guides to the source material are:
DONALDSON, GORDON, 'Sources for Scottish agrarian history before the eighteenth century', *Agricultural History Review*, vol. VIII, 1960, pp. 82–90.
DONALDSON, GORDON, 'Trends in rural history,' in *The Past and the Present: The Role of the National Museum of Antiquities of Scotland*, National Museum of Antiquities of Scotland, 1979, pp. 21–6.
SHAW, JOHN, 'Sources for Scottish agrarian history: part 1', *Scottish Local History*, no. 6, June 1985, pp. 18–24.
A bibliographical guide to theses is:

MORGAN, RAINE, *Dissertations on British Agrarian History: A Select List of Theses Awarded Higher Degrees in British and Foreign Universities Between 1876 and 1978*, University of Reading, 1981.
The Scottish Record Office holds a source list of its records relating to agrarian history.
The following works deal with the history of Scottish agriculture:
CARTER, I. R., *Farm Life in North East Scotland 1840–1914*, John Donald, 1979.
DODGSHON, R. A., *Land and Society in Early Scotland*, Oxford University Press, 1982.
FENTON, ALEXANDER, *Scottish Country Life*, John Donald, 1976.
FRANKLIN, T. B., *History of Scottish Farming*, Nelson, 1952 (this work is strongest on monastic farming).
HANDLEY, JAMES E., *The Agricultural Revolution in Scotland*, Burns, 1963.
HANDLEY, JAMES E., *Scottish Farming in the Eighteenth Century*, Faber, 1953.
SANDERSON, M. H. B., *Scottish Rural Society in the Sixteenth Century*, John Donald, 1982.
SINCLAIR, JOHN, *General Report on the Agricultural State and Political Circumstances of Scotland*, Board of Agriculture, 1814 (5 volumes).
WHYTE, I., *Agriculture and Society in Seventeenth Century Scotland*, John Donald, 1979.

Trade and industry

There is very full bibliographical coverage in this area:
MARWICK, WILLIAM HUTTON, 'A bibliography of works on Scottish economic history', *Economic History Review*, vol. III, no. 1, January 1931, pp. 117–37.
MARWICK, WILLIAM HUTTON, 'A bibliography of works on Scottish economic history published during the last twenty years', *Economic History Review*, 2nd series, vol. IV, no. 3, 1952, pp. 376–82.
MARWICK, WILLIAM HUTTON, 'A bibliography of Scottish economic history 1951–62,' *Economic History Review*, 2nd series, vol. V, no. 16, August 1963, pp. 147–54.
MARWICK, WILLIAM HUTTON, 'A bibliography of Scottish economic history during the last decade 1963–70', *Essays in Bibliography and Criticism*, vol. V, no. 67, 1973.
SCOTT, WILLIAM ROBERT, *Scottish Economic Literature to 1800*, Hodge, 1911.
An annual bibliography appears in the journal *Scottish Economic and Social History*
An important guide to sources, research methods and the bibliography of different industries is:
PAYNE, PETER L., *Studies in Scottish Business History*, Cass, 1967.
General studies on aspects of economic history are as follows:
CAMPBELL, R. H., *The Rise and Fall of Scottish Industry 1707–1939*, John Donald, 1980.
CAMPBELL, R. H., *Scotland Since 1707: The Rise of an Industrial Society*, Blackwell, 1965.
CAMPBELL, R. H. and DOW, J. B. A., *Source Book of Scottish Economic and Social History*, Blackwell, 1968.

GRANT, I. F., *The Economic History of Scotland*, Longman, Green & Co., 1934.

HAMILTON, HENRY, *The Industrial Revolution in Scotland*, Oxford University Press, 1932.

LYTHE, S. G. E. and BUTT, J., *An Economic History of Scotland 1100–1939*, Blackie, 1975.

MACKINNON, JAMES, *The Social and Industrial History of Scotland from the Earliest Times to the Union*, Blackie, 1920.

MARWICK, W. H., *Scotland in Modern Times: An Outline of Economic and Social Development since the Union of 1707*, Cass, 1964.

PAYNE, PETER L., *Early Scottish Limited Companies 1856–95*, Scottish Academic Press, 1981.

Scottish Industrial History, Scottish History Society, 1978.

A journal devoted to this field is *Scottish Industrial History*. Industry is one of the most extensively studied areas of Scottish history; there is no place here to mention the many works devoted to specific industries and firms. Relevant titles can be traced through the bibliographies listed above. Finally in this section, mention should be made of one of the most influential works of the last decade, in the study of all aspects of social and economic history:

SMOUT, T. C., *A History of the Scottish People 1560–1830*, 2nd edition, Collins, 1970.

Population

FLINN, M. W., *Scottish Population History*, Cambridge University Press, 1977.

Chapter 7. Writing and Publishing Results, pages 138–45

LEWIS, RAY and EASSON, JOHN B., *Publishing and Printing at Home*, David & Charles, 1984.

REFERENCES

ADAMS, I. H., 'Sources for Scottish local history – estate plans', *Local Historian*, vol. XII, 1976, pp. 26–30.

ANGUS, W., 'Charters, cartularies and deeds', in *Sources and Literature of Scots Law*, Stair Society, 1936, pp. 200–61.

ARMSTRONG, NORMA E. S., *Local Collections in Scotland*, Scottish Library Association, 1977.

CAMPBELL, R. H., 'The law and the joint-stock company in Scotland', in Payne, Peter L., *Studies in Scottish Business History*, Frank Cass, 1967, pp. 136–51.

COWAN, R. M. W., *The Newspaper in Scotland*, Outram, 1946.

FERGUSON, THOMAS, *The Dawn of Scottish Welfare*, Nelson, 1948.

FERGUSON, THOMAS, *Scottish Social Welfare 1864–1914*, E. & S. Livingstone, 1958.

FRANKLIN, T. B., *History of Scottish Farming*, Nelson, 1952.

FYFE, J. G., *Scottish Diaries and Memoirs 1550–1746*, Mackay, 1927.

FYFE, J. G., *Scottish Diaries and Memoirs 1746–1843*, Mackay, 1942.

GURNEY, JOSEPH JOHN, *Notes on Prisons and Prison Discipline*, Longman, 1819.

HAMILTON-EDWARDS, GERALD, *In Search of Scottish Ancestry*, 2nd edition, Phillimore, 1983.

MACFARLANE, ALAN, *Reconstructing Historical Communities*, Cambridge University Press, 1977.

MILL, A. J., *Inventory of the Records of the Older Scottish Burghs*, St Andrews University, 1923.

MITCHISON, ROSALIND, 'Sources for Scottish local history II – kirk session registers', *Local Historian*, vol. XI, 1974, pp. 229–35.

NEILD, JAMES, *State of the Prisons in England, Scotland and Wales . . .* , 1812.

OLIVER, GEORGE, 'Who held the camera? the Lind Collection', *Scots Magazine*, January 1980, pp. 406–17.

OLIVER, GEORGE, 'High days and holidays: the Lind Collection II', *Scots Magazine*, February 1980, pp. 500–6.

PRYDE, G. S., *Scotland from 1603 to the Present Day*, Nelson, 1962.

RAYNER, PATRICK, LENMAN, BRUCE and PARKER, GEOFFREY, *Handlist of Records for the Study of Crime in Early Modern Scotland*, Swift, 1983.

RICKARDS, MAURICE, *This is Ephemera*, David & Charles, 1977.

RIDEN, PHILIP, *Local History: A Handbook for Beginners*, Batsford, 1983.

ROBERTSON, D. and WOOD, M., 'Burgh Court Records', in *Sources and Literature of Scots Law*, Stair Society, 1936, pp. 104–10.

ST JOSEPH, J. K., *The Uses of Air Photography*, John Baker, 1977.

SMOUT, T. C., *A History of the Scottish People 1560–1830*, 2nd edition, Collins, 1970.

STUART, MARGARET, *Guide to Works of Reference on the History and*

Genealogy of Scottish Families, Oliver & Boyd, 1930.

THOMPSON, PAUL, *The Voice of the Past: Oral History*, Oxford University Press, 1978.

THOMSON, J. M., *The Public Records of Scotland*, Maclenox Jackson, 1922.

WAKE, JOAN, *How to Compile a History and Present Day Record of Village Life*, Federation of Women's Institutes, 1925.

WALKER, DAVID M., *The Scottish Legal System*, 5th edition, W. Green, 1981.

WHETSTONE, ANN E., *Scottish County Government in the Eighteenth and Nineteenth Centuries*, John Donald, 1981.

WHYTE, IAN, *Agriculture and Society in Seventeenth Century Scotland*, John Donald, 1979.

WHYTE, I. D. and WHYTE, K. A., *Sources for Scottish Historical Geography: An Introductory Guide*, Geo Abstracts, 1981.

WORMALD, JENNY, *Lords and Men in Scotland: Bonds of Manrent 1442–1603*, John Donald, 1985.

WORSLEY, PETER, *Introducing Sociology*, Penguin, 1970.

INDEX